SCOTLAND'S BEST
CASTLES AND STATELY HOMES

MARTIN COVENTRY

GOBLINSHEAD

First Edition 2014
© Martin Coventry 2014

Published by
GOBLINSHEAD

130B Inveresk Road, Musselburgh EH21 7AY, Scotland
Tel: 0131 665 2894 Email: goblinshead@sol.co.uk

British Library Cataloguing in Publication Data
A catalogue record for this book is available from
the British Library.

ISBN 9781899874576

Typeset by GOBLINSHEAD
Printed and bound in Glasgae by Bell & Bain

Disclaimer:
The factual information contained in this *Scotland's Best Castles and Stately Homes* (the "Material") is believed to be accurate at the time of printing, but no representation or warranty is given (express or implied) as to its accuracy, completeness or correctness. The author and publisher do not accept any liability whatsoever for any direct, indirect or consequential loss or damage arising in any way from any use of or reliance on this Material for any purpose.

While every care has been taken to compile and check all the information in this book, in a work of this complexity it is possible that mistakes and omissions may have occurred. If you know of any corrections, alterations or improvements, please contact the author or the publisher at the address above.

CONTENTS

ACKNOWLEDGMENTS

Many deep and warm thanks to everyone who provided photographs of sites or checked over the entries (copyright © of the images remains with the holders):

Beverley Rutherford for Abbotsford, for the image of Abbotsford (page C1) and the two images of Abbotsford (pages 1 & 2)

Fenella Corr for Ballindalloch Castle, images of Ballindalloch Castle and Ballindalloch Castle, Dining Room (page C2) and Ballindalloch Castle, Umbrella Hall (page 7)

Kate Hannah for Blair Castle, image of Blair Castle, Picture Staircase (page C4) and Blair Castle, Dining Room (page 13)

Sarah Peat and Helen Currie for Bowhill, image of Bowhill House, Dining Room (page C6) and image of Bowhill House, Stair Hall (page 18)

Doreen Wood for Braemar Castle, images of Braemar Castle and Braemar Castle, Dining Room (page C7)

Jane Hogg for Callendar House, image of Callendar House, Kitchen (page C9)

Shirley Farquhar for Castle of Mey, image of Castle of Mey (page C13) and images of Castle of Mey (page 41 & 42)

East Ayrshire Council for image of Dean Castle (page C20)

Joan Johnson for Delgatie Castle, for image of Delgatie Castle, painted ceiling (page C19) and images of Delgatie Castle (page 66 & 67)

Claire Oram for Drumlanrig Castle, for the four images of Drumlanrig Castle (pages C22 & 23) and image of Drumlanrig Castle, Dining Room (page 78)

Jess Higton and Andrew (Duart Guide) for Duart Castle, for the image of Duart Castle (top image) (page C25) and images of Duart Castle (page 81 & 82)

Charlotte Rostek for Dumfries House, for the image of Dumfries House, Pewter Corridor (page C26) and image of Dumfries House, Eagle Table (page 86)

Scott Morrison for Dunrobin Castle, for the image of Dunrobin Castle, Drawing Room (page C28)

David Win for Eilean Donan Castle (© DRW Photography), for the two images of Eilean Donan Castle (page C33) and the images of Eilean Donan Castle (pages 103 & 104)

Bob Lawson for Ferniehirst Castle, for the two images of Ferniehirst Castle (page C35)

Louise Rattray for Floors Castle, for the image of Floors Castle, Drawing Room (page C36)

Doreen Stout and Pauline for Glamis Castle, for the two images of Glamis Castle (page C38) and image of Glamis Castle, Chapel (page 118)

Suzan Caldwell and Piers de Salis for Hopetoun House, for the three images of Hopetoun House (page C42) and the image of Hopetoun House (page 128)

Jane Young for Inveraray Castle (© Argyll Estates/Hudson's Media Ltd), for the image of Inveraray Castle, State Dining Room (page C45) and the image of Inveraray Castle, Armoury Hall (page 138)

Jane Malloch for Mellerstain, for the four images of Mellerstain (pages C50 & C51)

Kathryn McLaughlin for Mount Stuart, for the three images of Mount Stuart (page C52 & C53 top) and image of Mount Stuart, Chapel (page 157)

Kara ter Morsche for Paxton House and Gunsgreen House, for the image of Gunsgreen House, blue panelled room (page C39), the image of Paxton House, Entrance Hall (page C56), the image of Gunsgreen House (page 120) and image of Paxton House, Old Kitchen (page 166)

Sarah Macdonald for Traquair House, for the image of Traquair House, Drawing Room (page C64) and the image of Traquair House, King's Room (page 195)

Gordon Mason for image of Bothwell Castle (page C5) and image of Bothwell Castle (page 14)

Aerial Shot of the Scottish Parliament (page 164) © Scottish Parliamentary Corporate Body – 2012. Licensed under the Open Scottish Parliament Licence v1.0.

Marcin Klimek at the Photo Library of The National Trust for Scotland (© National Trust for Scotland), for images of Craigievar Castle, Hall (page C14), Crathes Castle, Room of the Nine Nobles (page C16), Culzean Castle, Oval Staircase (page C18), Falkland Palace, tapestry in Chapel Royal (page C34), Fyvie Castle, Gallery (page C37), Haddo House (page C40), Hill of Tarvit, Dining Hall (page C41), Brodick Castle, Dining Room (page 23), Brodie Castle, Blue Sitting Room (page 25), Craigievar Castle,

The Blue Room (page 48), Crathes Castle, The Long Gallery (page 56), Culzean Castle, Circular Saloon (page 63), Falkland Palace, bedroom (page 108), Fyvie Castle, The Library (page 116), Haddo House (page 121 & 122), House of Dun (page 131), Newhailes, Dining Room (page 161) and The Binns (page 186)

All other photos (© Martin Coventry) by Martin Coventry, Joyce Miller or Dorothy Miller

Also thanks to Emma Begley at Historic Scotland, Luke Menzies for Castle Menzies, Wendy Sylvester for Dunnottar Castle, Lynne Leslie for Dunvegan Castle, Margaret Findlay for Lauriston Castle, Frances Reid for Thirlestane Castle, Cathy Ogg for Scone Palace and info@Cawdor Castle.

Huge thanks also to Joyce Miller and to Gordon Mason for reading over the text, and to Joyce Miller and Bill Coventry for coming along to visit all those castles, historic houses, royal palaces and stately homes this summer…hoping for many more castles and cakes in the following years.

INTRODUCTION

Although this book is called *Scotland's Best Castles and Stately Homes*, it should more accurately be called *Scotland's Best, in Joyce and Martin's Mostly Considered Opinion Having Visited Nearly All of Them, Castles, Historic Houses, Mansions, Royal Palaces and Stately Homes (and Their Cakes) which Are Open to the Public for At Least Some Weeks Regularly Each Year*. Not very catchy, though.

It is, of course, difficult to define what 'best' might mean in so many contexts. When first envisaged, I intended to feature no more than 50 castles and stately homes, starting from an initial list of 200 plus, which should have been easy to whittle down. How I intended to compare a grim ruined stronghold in a rugged spot to a beautifully proportioned classical mansion with a sumptuous and refined interior had not been considered, then. Even I, who prefer a crumbling stronghold, have been awestruck, overwhelmed, or even appalled, by some of the lavish interiors.

Perhaps it should be mentioned that with ruined castles you are seeing the bones of the building, stripped of decoration and ornament and furnishings, and that these great edifices were every bit as magnificent in their day as the grand stately homes of Scotland are now. Some ancient castles, of course, survived the age of strife and classicism, and retained or enhanced their baronial splendour.

I really tried but had only got to 85 places when I could find no more to cut. Indeed I had already dropped some of my favourite castles and houses, as sadly I could not find any category in which they were best. It was only the intervention of Joyce that stopped me going back and extending the list back to more than 100. So, it is true to say that I regret not including many more sites and there are some, with hindsight, I would have included, although I do not know which ones I would have dropped to give them space. There are also places I would have included had they been open on a more regular basis or if opening had not been uncertain.

Perhaps, indeed, 85 seems a lot to qualify as 'best', but in Scotland there were – at least at one time – thousands of castles and fortified houses, and then many more than a thousand mansions and stately homes which replaced these. And there are, of course, still hundreds of fantastic edifices in private hands, which are not open to the public.

The list is the best in my opinion, either outstanding places to visit and a great day out, pre-eminent examples of a particular style of architecture, the most romantic ruins in picturesque spots, or simply equipped with the most awe-inspiring and lavish interiors. We have, as ever, ended up with a larger book than first intended, extending the colour section from an emaciated sixteen pages to a robust and bouncing 64 pages with some 128 colour photos. All of the castles and houses are illustrated in colour and in black and white, and in many cases both inside and outside as well.

We had intended to visit all of the castles and houses in the book but for logistical reasons we did not manage to get to Ferniehirst Castle or to Castle of Mey. So they have been included blind, as it were. We will be rectifying this in 2014 and, as well as continuing to visit our favourite places, we will be going boldly to new, wonderful destinations. We have visited all the other places listed in the book, and have had many wonderful trips this summer, finally getting to those castles and houses we had missed for one reason or another. Luckily, it always seemed to be sunny. And most tearooms had cake.

So impressed were we with the millionaire's shortbread and carrot cake and Victoria sponge and macaroons, and lots of other delights, we were going to include a 'good cake index' for all the places. Sadly, after more reflection, we decided that it was too anecdotal and to compile properly would have entailed sampling all cakes at all sites. A challenge we might have been up to, but time was too short and our waistlines too bulging.

Most of these visits have been great, but over the years we have also had some that were not quite so good. Mostly we have tried not to let that colour our view of a place, as anyone can have an off day, however surly the waitress, numerous the bus tours, baffling the opening days and times, inadequate the sign posting – or why only lunch is served until 15.00 but not coffee or cake, even when the tearoom is only half full.

One especially irksome visit was to a certain large Adam mansion near Cumnock. After a difficult journey, finding the road closed at Douglas, we backtracked and then found ourselves going the wrong way east round the diversion and approaching Lanark. We also nearly got crushed by an HGV cutting a roundabout approaching the M74. With a trusty OS map (never leave home without one, although make sure it is up to date!) we navigated a way back west and eventually got to the entrance to the house. Then we found that Prince Charles had chosen that day to visit, and they were letting nobody in. So the not-very-helpful policemen informed us, not even being able to make a guess at when we would be let in. A member of staff there might have been helpful? Oh the joy. We were relatively civilized about it, but that could not be said for other would-be visitors backed up at the gates.

We did then have a lovely afternoon at Culzean Castle, and we returned to that said house near Cumnock and did have a great visit after all. No royal disruption that time!

Another disturbing time, perhaps with a ghostly element, was had during my second visit to Craignethan Castle. I was wearing shorts. Disturbing enough in itself, but while using the little men's room I had a bizarre episode with my newly purchased guidebook and the toilet seat. The loo seat would not stay up so I put my guidebook on the cistern. Only my guidebook would not stay on the cistern, no matter how carefully I placed it, and began to slip off. With no way to hold both the guide book and the loo seat, my guide book ended up in the pan. Possibly a playful ghost...

In this day and age it might be thought it would be difficult to get lost when on a visit to a popular house to the south of Glasgow. This time we were defeated by a lack of signs and an overly thrifty approach to replacing maps. We were gaily driving along the M8, from the west, but somehow missed the turn off, despite it being the M77. So on we went, junction after junction, getting more and more frustrated. Out came the trusty OS map and then I navigated us round the south-east side of Glasgow, only to find the map was 20 years old and that new roads had been built and others renumbered. If we had been trying to find the National Museum of Rural Life, we could not have gone wrong as there were signs at every junction, but was there a sign for our destination, nope, nary a one. Finally the OS map came into its own and we found our way to the park and to the house. I then bought some new maps, cursing the cost and the non-existent signage.

These new maps were useful for navigating our way out of Kilmarnock.

Overall, though, during the past 20 years Joyce and I, and also Bill for many visits, have had few disasters and many many wonderful days, some so good or with so much laughter that it was actually painful when they finished and the house and cafe and shop and gates were shutting, the day was over and the sun was setting – and the half-cooked baked potato I had had for lunch was fighting a valiant rear-guard action.

Anyway we hope you have as many wonderful visits as we have had, and that this book is as much fun to use as it was to compile.

Martin Coventry
Musselburgh, December 2013

MAP OF THE NORTH OF SCOTLAND

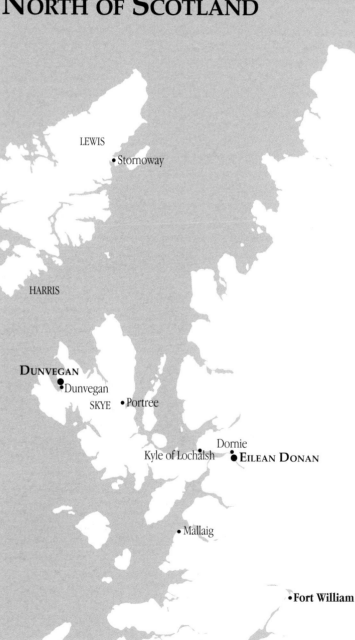

LEWIS
• Stornoway

HARRIS

DUNVEGAN
• Dunvegan
SKYE • Portree

Dornie
Kyle of Lochalsh • EILEAN DONAN

• Mallaig

• Fort William

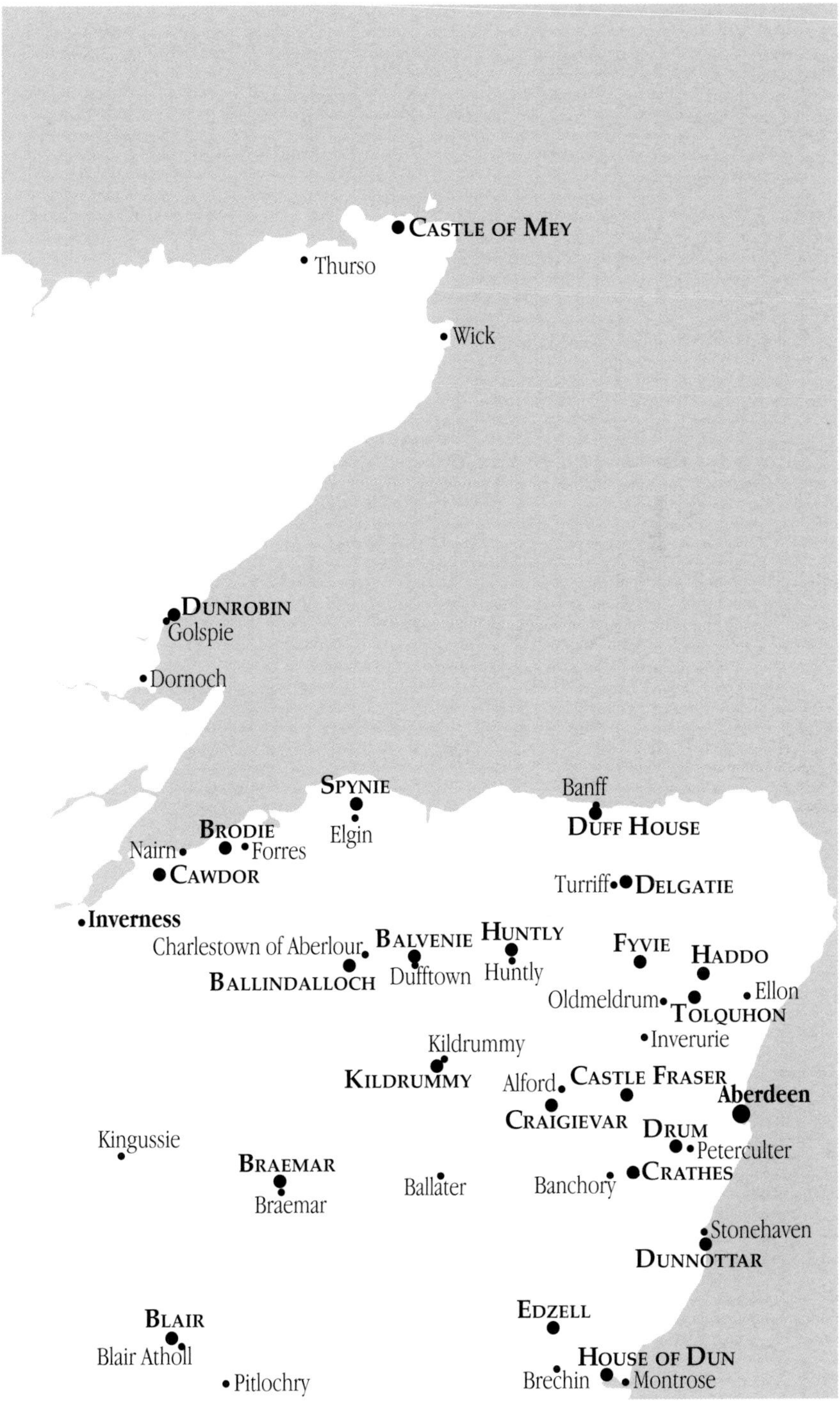

CASTLE OF MEY

Thurso

Wick

DUNROBIN
Golspie

Dornoch

SPYNIE
Banff

BRODIE Elgin **DUFF HOUSE**
Nairn **Forres**
CAWDOR
Turriff **DELGATIE**

Inverness
Charlestown of Aberlour **BALVENIE HUNTLY** **FYVIE HADDO**
BALLINDALLOCH Dufftown Huntly
Oldmeldrum **TOLQUHON** Ellon

Kildrummy Inverurie

KILDRUMMY Alford **CASTLE FRASER**
Aberdeen

Kingussie **CRAIGIEVAR DRUM**
Peterculter
BRAEMAR **CRATHES**
Ballater Banchory
Braemar

Stonehaven
DUNNOTTAR

BLAIR **EDZELL**
Blair Atholl
HOUSE OF DUN
Pitlochry Brechin Montrose

xi

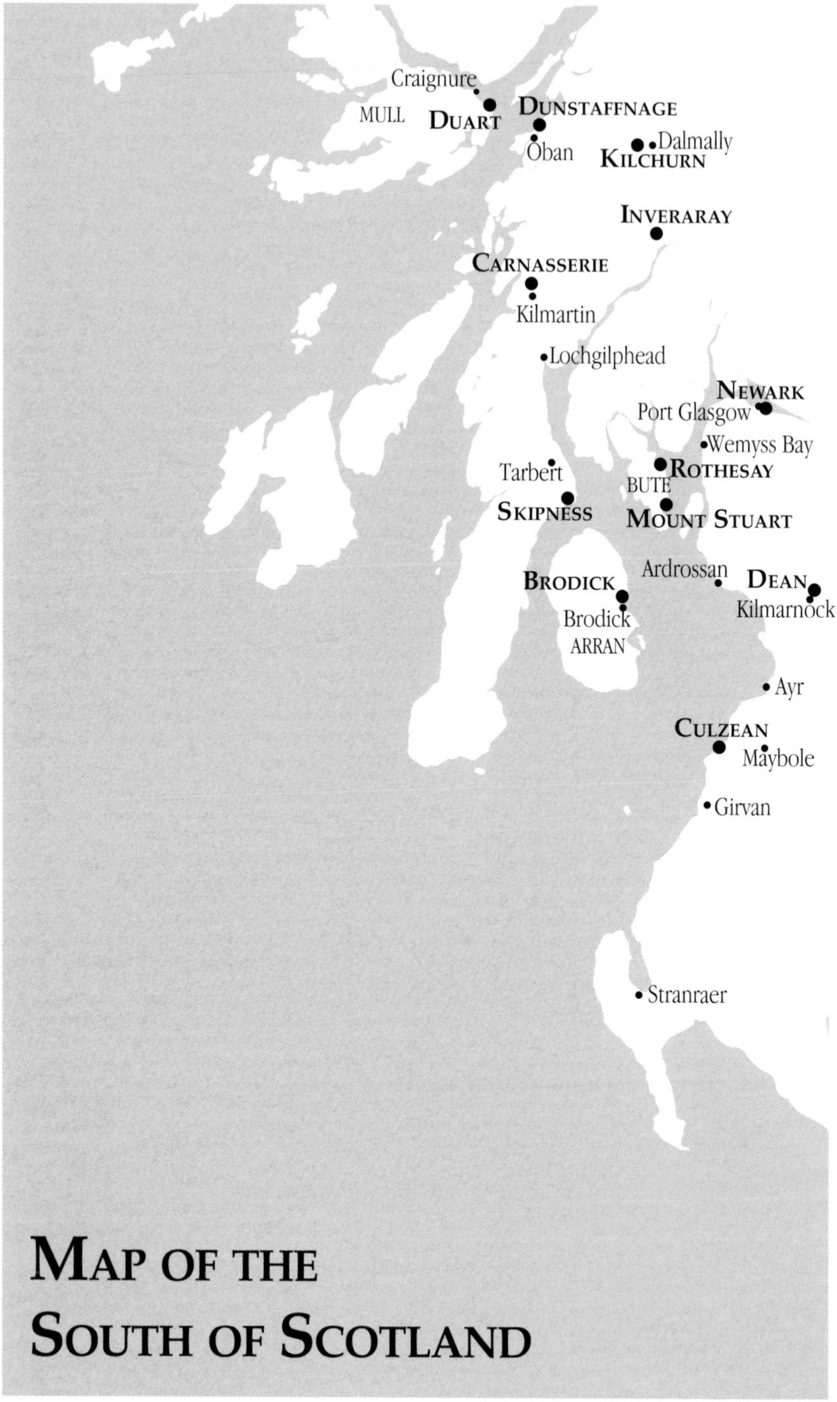

Craignure
MULL **DUART** **DUNSTAFFNAGE**
Oban **KILCHURN** •Dalmally

INVERARAY

CARNASSERIE
Kilmartin
•Lochgilphead

NEWARK
Port Glasgow
•Wemyss Bay
Tarbert **ROTHESAY**
BUTE
SKIPNESS **MOUNT STUART**

BRODICK Ardrossan **DEAN**
Brodick Kilmarnock
ARRAN

• Ayr

CULZEAN
Maybole

•Girvan

• Stranraer

MAP OF THE
SOUTH OF SCOTLAND

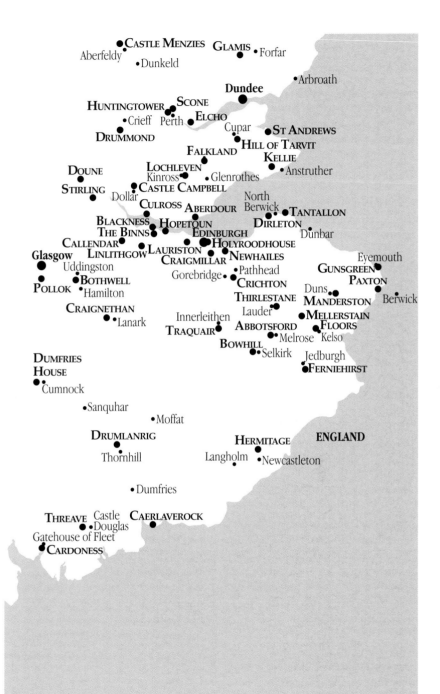

Aberfeldy ●CASTLE MENZIES GLAMIS ●Forfar
●Dunkeld

●Arbroath

Dundee
●

HUNTINGTOWER ●SCONE
●Crieff Perth ●ELCHO
Cupar
DRUMMOND ●ST ANDREWS
FALKLAND HILL OF TARVIT
KELLIE
DOUNE LOCHLEVEN ●Anstruther
Kinross● ●Glenrothes
STIRLING ●CASTLE CAMPBELL
Dollar North
CULROSS ABERDOUR Berwick ●TANTALLON
BLACKNESS HOPETOUN DIRLETON
THE BINNS● EDINBURGH Dunbar
CALLENDAR LAURISTON HOLYROODHOUSE
Glasgow LINLITHGOW CRAIGMILLAR ●NEWHAILES Eyemouth
● Uddingston ●Pathhead GUNSGREEN●
Gorebridge● CRICHTON PAXTON
POLLOK ●BOTHWELL Duns ● Berwick
●Hamilton THIRLESTANE MANDERSTON
CRAIGNETHAN Lauder● ●MELLERSTAIN
●Lanark Innerleithen ABBOTSFORD FLOORS
TRAQUAIR● ●●Melrose Kelso
BOWHILL ●●Selkirk Jedburgh
DUMFRIES ●FERNIEHIRST
HOUSE
●●Cumnock

●Sanquhar
●Moffat

DRUMLANRIG HERMITAGE ENGLAND
●
Thornhill Langholm ●Newcastleton

●Dumfries

THREAVE Castle CAERLAVEROCK
●●Douglas ●
Gatehouse of Fleet
●CARDONESS

xiii

HOW TO USE THE BOOK

The main part of the book is organized alphabetically, featuring some 85 castles, mansions, historic houses, royal palaces and stately homes, beginning with Abbotsford and ending with Traquair House.

Each entry has a thumbnail map, page number reference (C1, C2 etc) to the photos in the colour section, description of the place, history, development and ownership, stories about ghosts or hauntings, and one or more black-and-white photos, both exterior and interior shots.

Following this, in the shaded box, is information on location and distance from main Scottish cities, with National Grid Reference (NGR), Ordnance Survey (OS) Landranger number, and post code.

There are then details of opening, and whether the site is managed by Historic Scotland (HS) or The National Trust for Scotland (NTS). This information has all been checked, directly with places or with their websites, but should not be relied upon, as information can change or be updated at short notice.

Then a brief list of facilities and disabled access is given, and following this are the five nearest places with shortest distances by road.

The colour section is also mostly organized alphabetically, but because some places have more than one photo, indeed as many as four photos, this is not always the case. There are photos of both the exterior and the interior for many places.

The acknowledgments section at the beginning (page iv-vi) attributes all the photos.

There are maps locating all the sites on page x-xiii.

There is a glossary of architectural terms used on page 197, followed by brief descriptions of titles and offices on page 201.

The index, on the final pages 205-206, lists all the castles, mansions, palaces and houses featured, with the page number in both the main part of the text and in the colour section, and whether the site is managed by Historic Scotland (HS) or the NTS.

NOTES

• The distances between places given in the text is the shortest route by car, NOT as the crow flies. This can be significantly different, especially in Highland or remote areas. Many places can be reached by public transport but, if not in major cities or populated areas, this usually takes some planning and blind faith in a deity.

• Locations on maps are for general guidance only.

- Opening dates and times have been checked with all the places or against their websites. If travelling any distance, however, it is strongly recommended that you check opening details with the places you intend to visit, preferably by phone (you never know when Prince Charles is going to drop in) or by checking websites (although these are not always accurate).

- Opening dates are inclusive, so Apr-Sep in the text means open from 1 April to 30 September. Opening dates may vary from year to year, especially because many places open for the moveable feast of Easter or may be open for only part of the week. It should be assumed that all sites with winter opening are closed for 25-26 December and 1-2 January. Edinburgh Castle, the Palace of Holyroodhouse and Stirling Castle are open at New Year (although closed on 25-26 Dec). There do not appear to be any other manned sites that are.

- If a member of your party has a disability, check with sites before visiting. Disabled access referred to in the shaded box is for wheelchair access and can only be brief as the arrangements at many sites are too complicated to explain. Castles, of course, are designed not to be easily accessed, even by the physically able.

- Please note that the opening of some sites is weather dependant, especially in the winter months.

- Post codes can be useful for SatNavs but may only go close to the site – or may direct to a closed gate... Virtually all the castles and houses mentioned are signposted from main roads, although this is by no means always done well. If in doubt get an up-to-date OS map.

- Although some of the places featured in this book offer free entry, virtually all charge admission fees. For most smaller manned Historic Scotland sites this is around £5 each, for most houses and larger sites around £10, for Edinburgh and Stirling Castles as much as £16. Family tickets are often available, as are concessions, and also see below.

  Bearing this in mind, however, it is prudent not to arrive late in the day when visiting expensive sites. In other words, a bit of planning may save a few pounds. Many places, as well as a visit or tour, offer walks through the gardens and grounds, shopping outlets, distractions such as falconry displays or archery, museums and much much else.

- If you intend to visit many Historic Scotland and NTS sites (or their equivalents in England) it is recommended that you join these organizations, although of course there is a fee to join. Along with other benefits, you get free entry to places which have admission charges, some of which are otherwise very expensive. And in the second year free entry to the equivalent bodies in England, English Heritage and the National Trust. Contact details are:

Historic Scotland (HS)

Longmore House, Salisbury Place, Edinburgh EH9 1SH
Tel: 0131 668 8800
Web: www.historic-scotland.gov.uk

The National Trust for Scotland (NTS)

Wemyss House, 28 Charlotte Square, Edinburgh EH2 4ET
Tel: 0131 243 9300
Web: www.nts.org.uk

Historic Scotland and NTS sites can be rented for weddings and other events.

The Historic Houses Association may also be of interest, as paid membership allows free entry to some 300 houses, castles and gardens throughout Scotland and the UK, along with other benefits. Contact details are:

Historic Houses Association

2 Chester Street, London
SW1X 7BB
Tel: 020 7259 5688
Web: www.hha.org.uk

- Detailed guidebooks are usually available from manned sites.

- Sensible footwear and rainwear is usually advisable, whether climbing endless worn turnpike stairs,

trudging along miles of paths to brooding castles or round gardens and through bogle-infested woods.

- Midge repellent may also be advisable, especially on the west coast. Avon Skin So Soft is recommended: it does seem to work, and then, afterwards, skin is also so soft…The smell of summer.

- Take some iron rations: water and food. Some places do run out of provender, even at lunchtime, especially when coach parties have arrived unannounced or when the mains water gets cut off.

- Take a good torch. Some ruined castles are dimly lit (if at all).

- Almost all (and probably all, were they known) castles and large houses have or have had ghost or spooky stories associated with them. These stories should be taken for what they are: imaginative and often heavily embroidered tales. Castles and historic houses have often been inhabited for hundreds of year. People lived quite happily with any reputed ghost, imagined or not, for this time. In other words, ghosts may or may not exist but do not overly worry about a haunting as reported manifestations, what-ever TV shows purport to show, are exceptionally rare – if they occur at all.

- Many places have truly delicious cakes: these should be eaten without moderation…

SCOTLAND'S BEST
CASTLES AND STATELY HOMES

ABBOTSFORD

Colour photos page C1

In a lovely location by the banks of the River Tweed, Abbotsford is a fine baronial mansion with turrets, battlements and corbiestepped gables, and dates from the first quarter of the 19th century.

Sir Walter Scott, the famous Scottish writer, poet, sheriff and historian, bought Cartley Hole farmhouse, by the Tweed, in 1812, which he renamed Abbotsford. He had the old house demolished in 1822, and it was replaced by the main block of Abbotsford as it is today.

Scott was the most successful author of his day, and wrote many works including *Ivanhoe*, *Rob Roy*, the *Waverley* Novels and the *Lay of the Last Minstrel* – he was also responsible for the rediscovery of the Scottish Crown Jewels, which has been long hidden in Edinburgh Castle. Scott also collected many historic artefacts, and there is an impressive collection of armour and weapons at the house, including Rob Roy MacGregor's gun, a crucifix of Mary Queen of Scots, Graham of Claverhouse's pistol and the Marquis of Montrose's sword.

There is access to Scott's study, library, drawing room, entrance hall and armouries, as well as the dining room, where Scott died in 1832. His library of more than 9000 rare volumes is preserved at the house.

There are also extensive gardens and grounds, and a private chapel which was added after Scott's death.

Abbotsford

1

Abbotsford, Library

The ghost of Sir Walter Scott is said to haunt the dining room, where he died in 1832 after exhausting himself trying to pay off a huge debt. Sightings of his apparition have been reported in recent times.

35 mile south-east of Edinburgh, 72 miles east and south of Glasgow, 3 miles west of Melrose, off B6360, by River Tweed, at Abbotsford (signposted).
NT 508343 OS: 73 TD6 9BQ
Open all year: Apr-Sep, daily 10.00-1700; Oct-Mar, daily 10.00-16.00; closed 25/26 Dec and 1/2 Jan. Venue for weddings and events. Luxury self-catering accommodation.
Tel: 01896 752043 Web: www.scottsabbotsford.co.uk
Features: Parking. Visitor centre. Gift shop. Restaurant. WC. Walled and Morris Garden. Woodland walk. Adventure playground. Admission charged.
Nearest:
Bowhill House (7 miles)
Mellerstain (13 miles)
Thirlestane Castle (14 miles)
Floors Castle (15 miles)
Traquair House (16 miles)

ABERDOUR CASTLE

Colour photo page C1

I n the attractive village by the railway station, Aberdour Castle is a partly ruinous E-plan tower house, with a ruinous altered 12th- or 13th-century hall house and later wings and extensions, some of which are complete. The hall house may be one of the oldest standing stone castles in Scotland. Buildings, including a bakehouse and brewhouse block, were added in the 16th century, and about 1630 the castle was extended by a block occupied on the first floor by a gallery. One of the chambers in this range has an original painted ceiling, dating from the early 17th century.

The castle had a walled courtyard, of which a round turret survives. A terraced garden has been restored and there is an orchard and a beehive doocot, which dates from the 16th century and was still in use in 1746. There is also a fine walled garden with many scented plants.

This was a property of the Mortimer family, one of whom gave his name to Mortimer's Deep, the stretch of water between Inch Colm and Aberdour, after his coffin was cast overboard there. One story has Mortimer being a wicked fellow and, despite leaving land to the abbey, the monks did not want him buried on Inch Colm and on the journey a storm blew up and Mortimer's remains were washed overboard; another that the monks themselves were wicked and money-grasping, and cast his coffin into the sea.

Aberdour was a possession of Thomas Randolph, a friend and captain of

Aberdour Castle

Aberdour Castle, Gallery

Robert the Bruce, by 1325, but in 1342 the property passed to the Douglases, who were made Earls of Morton about 1456. James Douglas, 4th Earl of Morton, was made Regent Morton for the young James VI in 1572, although in 1581 he was executed for his alleged part in the murder of Darnley, the second husband of Mary, Queen of Scots. Much of the castle had been abandoned by 1725, by when the family had moved to nearby Aberdour House, although one wing of the old castle may have been occupied by Robert Watson of Muirhouse until his death in 1791. Part of the castle had been burnt out in 1715, and much of the hall house block collapsed in 1844 and then again in 1919, while the range with the gallery was used as a barracks, school room, masonic hall and dwelling until 1924, when the castle was put into the care of State.

The adjacent church of St Fillan's, which later became the parish church, dates from the 12th century, although it was much altered in the 17th. It stands in a lovely peaceful spot, is open to the public, and the burial ground has many interesting memorials. Aberdour is a scenic village and the harbour, beaches and Hawkcraig Point are particularly picturesque.

18 miles north of Edinburgh, 44 miles east and north of Glasgow, 3 miles west of Burntisland, in Aberdour, by railway station, off A921, Aberdour Castle (signposted).
NT 193854 OS: 66 KY3 0SL
Historic Scotland: Open Apr-Sep, daily 9.30-17.30; Oct-Mar, Sat-Wed

Aberdour Castle

9.30-16.30, closed Thu-Fri; cafe closes 60 mins before castle; last ticket 30 mins before closing; closed 25/26 Dec and 1/2 Jan.
Tel: 01383 860519 Web: www.historic-scotland.gov.uk
Features: Parking. Gift shop. Cafe. WC. Disabled access to ground floor (tea room), walled garden and upper terraces. Walled and terraced garden. Picnic area. Admission charged. Venue for weddings and events.
Nearest:
Hopetoun House (12 miles)
The Binns (14 miles)
Blackness Castle (15 miles)
Lauriston Castle (15 miles)
Lochleven Castle (15 miles)

BALLINDALLOCH CASTLE

Colour photos page C2

Inverness
BALLINDALLOCH
Charlestown
of Aberlour
Aberdeen

In fine gardens and grounds, Ballindalloch Castle is an impressive, attractive and homely Z-plan tower house, which dates from the 16th century. The oldest part consists of a main block with towers projecting at opposite corners. A round stair-tower in the middle of one front is crowned by a square watch-chamber. The walls of the tower are pierced by shot-holes and small windows. The castle was transformed in the 18th and 19th centuries into an elegant and comfortable residence.

The lands originally belonged to the Ballindalloch family, but passed to the Grants by 1499. The story goes that work began on the castle at another site, but any building was quickly dismantled, reputedly by fairies. A voice was heard telling that the castle should be moved and the present site was chosen.

The castle was captured and sacked by the Gordons during a feud, and was burned by the Marquis of Montrose after the Battle of Inverlochy in 1645. In the 18th century, the property passed by marriage to the Macphersons. The house is still occupied by the Macpherson-Grants and, among many other attractions, has an extensive collection of 17th-century Spanish paintings.

A Green Lady has reputedly been seen in the dining room, and reports of a Pink Lady are also recorded. Another ghost is said to be that of General James

Ballindalloch Castle

Ballindalloch Castle, Umbrella Hall

Grant, who died in 1806. Grant was very proud of the improvements he had made to the estate, and his phantom is said to ride around the lands every night to survey his achievement. He is then said to go into the wine cellar.

Another ghost, reportedly seen at the nearby Bridge of Avon, is that of a girl believed to have been unlucky in love.

138 miles north of Edinburgh, 47 miles east and south of Inverness, 8 miles south-west of Charlestown of Aberlour, on A95, at Ballindalloch Castle (signposted).
NJ 178365   OS: 28   AB37 9AX
Open Good Fri-Sep, Sun-Fri 10.30-last admission 16.45, closed Sat; other times by appt. Venue for weddings and events.
Tel: 01807 500205   Web: www.ballindallochcastle.co.uk
Features: Parking. Shop. Tea room. WC. Disabled access to ground floor and grounds. Gardens and grounds. Grass labyrinth. River walks. Admission charged.
Nearest:
Balvenie Castle (13 miles)
Spynie Palace (25 miles)
Brodie Castle (26 miles)
Huntly Castle (27 miles)
Cawdor Castle (40 miles)

BALVENIE CASTLE

Colour photo page C3

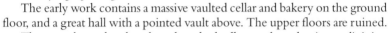

I n a pleasant and peaceful location, Balvenie Castle is a large ruinous courtyard castle. The oldest part is the strong 13th-century curtain wall and surrounding ditch, to which was added an L-plan tower house of four storeys at one corner, and other 15th-century now ruined ranges. The walls are pierced by gunloops.

The entrance, still with the original yett, is flanked by a projecting round tower.

The early work contains a massive vaulted cellar and bakery on the ground floor, and a great hall with a pointed vault above. The upper floors are ruined.

The tower house has three barrel-vaulted cellars, and another in an adjoining tower, which has a fine chamber on the first floor over the entrance pend.

The Comyn Earls of Buchan built the first castle, then called Mortlach, which was sacked by the forces of Robert the Bruce in 1308; Edward I of England had visited in 1304. Balvenie passed to the Douglases, who rebuilt the castle, but was granted to John Stewart, Earl of Atholl, by James II following the fall of the Black Douglases in 1455. Mary, Queen of Scots, probably visited in 1562.

In 1614 Balvenie was sold to Robert Innes of Invermarkie, and the family were made Baronets of Nova Scotia in 1628. The castle was used by the Marquis of Montrose during his campaign against the Covenanters in 1644-5. It was

Balvenie Castle, courtyard and tower house

Balvenie Castle, curtain wall

near here that a Covenanter force, led by Alexander Leslie, defeated a Royalist army in 1649, taking 900 prisoners. The Innes family suffered much by supporting the Royalist side in the Civil War, and had to sell the property to the Duffs of Braco in 1687. The castle was held by the Jacobites in 1689, but in 1715 was held against them by the Duffs.

Balvenie was not occupied after William Duff committed suicide here in 1718, and was soon unroofed – although a Hanoverian force, under the Duke of Cumberland, briefly held it in 1746.

The castle is said to be haunted by a White Lady, and a groom with two horses among other manifestations.

The village was originally known as Mortlach, but was named Dufftown after being rebuilt by the Duff Earl of Fife in the 19th century. There are several whisky distilleries in or near Dufftown, including the Glenfiddich distillery.

166 miles north of Edinburgh, 52 miles north-west of Aberdeen, 60 miles east of Inverness, 0.5 miles north of Dufftown, off B975 just east of junction with A941, at Balvenie Castle (signposted).
NJ 326409 OS: 28 AB55 4DH
Historic Scotland: open Apr-Sep, daily 9.30-17.30.
Tel: 01340 820121 Web: www.historic-scotland.gov.uk
Features: Parking. Shop. WC. Picnic area. Admission charged.
Nearest:
Ballindalloch Castle (13 miles)
Huntly Castle (15 miles)
Spynie Palace (20 miles)
Kildrummy Castle (23 miles)
Brodie Castle (31 miles)

BLACKNESS CASTLE

Colour photo page C3

On an outcrop of rock on a promontory in the Firth of Forth, Blackness is a grim and impressive courtyard castle, which was used as a state prison.

The entrance has an iron yett of 1693, and is protected by a spur with caponier and gun platforms. It leads into the courtyard, the curtain wall dating partly from the 15th century, although it was massively strengthened for artillery in the 16th and 17th centuries.

The oldest part is the central square 15th-century tower of four storeys, heightened in 1553, and altered again with the addition of a projecting round stair-tower. This was used as a prison for nobles, each chamber having a fireplace and latrine.

The landward tower is probably the site of the 15th-century hall, but the present building, dating mostly from 1540, housed the main residential accommodation for the castle. The sea tower served as an artillery platform, and as a secondary prison, a hatch giving access to a pit-prison which was open to the sea at high tide. There are fine views from the walls.

In medieval times, Blackness was an important port for the royal burgh of

Blackness Castle

Linlithgow, although it declined after the emergence of Bo'ness in the 17th century. The castle is first mentioned as a prison in 1449. In the 15th century Blackness was acquired by George Crichton, brother of the Chancellor of Scotland. During the reign of James II in 1444, the Douglases seized and sacked the castle, but it was quickly recovered by the Crichtons. In 1453 Sir George Crichton stopped his son, James, inheriting the property. James captured Blackness Castle, and imprisoned his father until forced to surrender by the king.

The castle was burned by an English fleet in 1481. From 1537, under Sir James Hamilton of Finnart – builder of Craignethan Castle – work began to turn the castle into an artillery fort, making it one of the most formidable fortresses in Scotland at that time. In 1543 Cardinal David Beaton was imprisoned here, and the following year Archibald Douglas, 6th Earl of Angus, although both were released. When Mary, Queen of Scots, fled to England in 1568 the castle held out for her until 1573.

The castle was captured by Cromwell's forces in 1650, being bombarded by land and sea, but most damage was done by a battery placed on the high ground on the landward side. The castle was not repaired until 1660, when it was used as a prison again. In the 19th century, Blackness was greatly altered to hold powder and stores, and became the central ammunition depot for Scotland. In 1912 the castle was handed over to the care of the State, restored, and is now in the care of Historic Scotland. The castle was a location in the movie *Hamlet* with Mel Gibson and BBC TV's *Ivanhoe*.

It is said that there is an underground passage from Blackness to The Binns, which is more than a mile away.

16 miles west of Edinburgh, 39 miles east and north of Glasgow, 4 miles east and north of Linlithgow, on the south shore of the Firth of Forth, off B903, east of the village of Blackness, at Blackness Castle (signposted).
NT 056803   OS: 65   EH49 7NH
Historic Scotland: open Apr-Sep, daily 9.30-7.30; Oct-Mar, Sat-Wed 9.30-16.30; closed Thu & Fri; closed 25/26 Dec and 1/2 Jan; last ticket sold 30 mins before closing.
Tel: 01506 834807 Web: www.historic-scotland.gov.uk
Features: Parking. Shop. Refreshments. WC. Picnic area. Limited disabled access. Admission charged.
Nearest:
The Binns (2 miles)
Linlithgow Palace (4 miles)
Hopetoun House (9 miles (by road))
Callendar House (12 miles)
Lauriston Castle (13 miles)

11

BLAIR CASTLE

Colour photos page C4

Standing in a beautiful mountainous location in a extensive estate, Blair Castle is a fairytale rambling mansion with towers, turrets, battlements and whitewashed walls. The castle incorporates the 13th-century Comyn's Tower, but the building was then added to through the centuries, then completely remodelled in the 18th century. In 1872 the Duke of Atholl had the architect David Bryce restore the look of the building back to the original. The castle stands in acres of attractive parkland and grounds, and there is a huge walled garden with colourful borders, ponds and a canal.

The castle has a sumptuous interior with a flourish of 18th century plasterwork in the imposing dining room and grand drawing room.

Edward III of England stayed at the castle in 1336, as did James V in 1529 and Mary, Queen of Scots, in 1564. In 1629 Blair was granted to John Murray, Master of Tullibardine, after he had married an heiress to the lands, and he became Earl of Atholl. In 1653 the castle was besieged, captured and partly destroyed with powder by Colonel Daniel, one of Cromwell's commanders. However, it was complete enough for the young Earl of Atholl to try to recapture it in 1654. The castle was garrisoned by Bonnie Dundee, John Graham of Claverhouse, in 1689, and it was here that his body was brought after the Battle of Killiecrankie. The Earls of Atholl were made Marquises, then Dukes of Atholl in 1703, and gained the sovereignty of the Isle of Man in 1736,

Blair Castle

Blair Castle, Dining Room

which they held to 1765 when it was given to the Crown.

Bonnie Prince Charlie stayed at Blair in 1745, during the Rising. The following year the castle was held by Hanoverian forces, and it was attacked and damaged by Lord George Murray, Bonnie Prince Charlie's general and the Duke's brother. It is the last castle in Britain to have been besieged.

Robert Burns visited in 1787, as did Queen Victoria. Blair Castle is home to the Atholl Highlanders, Britain's only remaining private regiment.

The castle is said to have a Grey Lady, that glides about silently.

77 miles north and west of Edinburgh, 35 miles north and west of Perth, 7 miles north of Pitlochry, 1 mile north-west of Blair Atholl, off B8079 from A9, at Blair Castle (signposted).
NN 867662 OS: 43 PH18 5TL
Open Apr-Oct, daily 9.30-17.30, last admission 15.30; also wknds leading up to Xmas for Xmas activities. Venue for weddings, events and functions. Country sports. Self-catering accommodation available on estate.
Tel: 01796 481207 Web: www.blair-castle.co.uk
Features: Parking. Shop. Restaurant. WC. Disabled access to ground floor & facilities. Walled garden. Admission charged.
Castle Menzies (23 miles)
Scone Palace (36 miles)
Drummond Castle Gardens (46 miles)
Glamis Castle (47 miles)
Braemar Castle (47 miles)

BOTHWELL CASTLE

Colour photo page C5

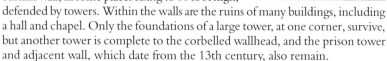

Bothwell Castle is one of the largest and finest stone castles in Scotland, and stands in a lovely location above the River Clyde. One notable feature is the ruin of the magnificent moated round donjon, which stands at one end of the courtyard.

The courtyard is enclosed by a strong thick curtain wall, in some places rising to 60 foot high, defended by towers. Within the walls are the ruins of many buildings, including a hall and chapel. Only the foundations of a large tower, at one corner, survive, but another tower is complete to the corbelled wallhead, and the prison tower and adjacent wall, which date from the 13th century, also remain.

The magnificent donjon has a surrounding ditch partly hewn out of rock, 25 foot wide and 15 foot deep. The entrance to the donjon is through a fine pointed doorway, originally reached by a drawbridge across the ditch. The entrance, through a portcullis, led into a passage to the hall. There is a turnpike

Bothwell Castle, ruin of donjon

Bothwell Castle, courtyard

stair to the basement with a well. Half of the donjon was destroyed in the 14th century.

Due to its position, size and strength, Bothwell Castle was of major importance during the Wars of Independence, and it was a property of the Murrays from the middle of the 13th century, having passed by marriage from the Oliphants. The castle was held by the English in 1298-9, but was besieged by the Scots and eventually taken after 14 months. In 1301 Edward I recaptured the castle, and it became the headquarters of Aymer de Valence, Earl of Pembroke, Edward I's Warden of Scotland. It was surrendered to the Scots in 1314, and the donjon was partly demolished at this time. The captain of the castle was called de Homildon from his property in Northumberland, but was given lands at Cadzow for his service by Robert the Bruce, and so started the Hamiltons.

In 1336 the castle was taken and rebuilt by the English, and Edward III of England made Bothwell his headquarters, but it was soon demolished again after recapture by the Scots, led by Sir Andrew Murray. The last Murray laird died from plague about 1360.

In 1362 it was acquired by marriage by Archibald the Grim, 3rd Earl of Douglas and Lord of Galloway, and he rebuilt much of the castle. After the forfeiture of the Black Douglases in 1455, the castle eventually went to Patrick Hepburn of Dunsyre, Lord Hailes, later Earl of Bothwell, who exchanged Bothwell for Hermitage Castle with the Douglases in 1492. James IV visited Bothwell in 1503 and 1504.

In the 17th century Archibald Douglas, 1st Earl of Forfar, built a classical mansion – demolished in 1926 because of subsidence due to coal mining – near the castle, dismantling part of the old stronghold for materials.

Bothwell Castle, ruin of donjon from courtyard

Bonnie Jean reputedly haunts the castle, and on Halloween is said to appear above the donjon. She fell in love with a local lad, and they decided to elope. She was sailing across the Clyde to meet her paramour, when a storm blew up, her boat sank and the poor love-struck lass drowned.

11 miles east of Glasgow, 39 miles east and south of Edinburgh, 3 miles north and west of Hamilton, off B7071, east bank of River Clyde, 1 mile south-west of Uddingston, at Bothwell Castle (signposted).
NS 688594 OS: 64 G71 8BL
Historic Scotland: open Apr-Sep, daily 9.30-17.30; Oct-Mar, Sat-Wed 9.30-16.30, closed Thu & Fri; closed 25/26 Dec and 1/2 Jan; last ticket sold 30 mins before closing. Short walk to castle.
Tel: 01698 816894 Web: www.historic-scotland.gov.uk
Features: Parking. Gift shop. Refreshments. WC. Limited disabled access. Picnic area. Admission charged.
Pollok House (13 miles)
Craignethan Castle (16 miles)
Callendar House (22 miles)
Dean Castle (27 miles)
Linlithgow Palace (29 miles)

Bowhill House

Colour photos page C6

Set in many acres of landscaped and wooded grounds, Bowhill is an extensive rambling mansion, dating mainly from 1812, although part may be from 1708. The house was remodelled in 1831-2 by the architects William Burn and David Bryce, and has a magnificent interior.

There are fine collections of paintings by artists such as Canaletto, Raeburn, Reynolds and Gainsborough and artefacts including the Duke of Monmouth's saddle and execution shirt. There are formal gardens at the front of the house.

The lands were held by the Scotts from the 16th century or earlier, but were sold to the Murrays around 1690 and they built a house here. In 1747, the property was bought by Francis Scott, 2nd Duke of Buccleuch, so that his son Lord Charles could stand for parliament. Bowhill remains with his descendants, and Sir Walter Scott, who built nearby Abbotsford, was a frequent visitor, describing the house as 'Sweet Bowhill' in his poem *The Lay of the Last Minstrel*.

The house was used as a military hospital during World War I, and then by the army between 1939-45. The house had deteriorated during the war and because of dry rot, but has since been restored to its former glory.

Bowhill House

Bowhill House, Stair Hall

S tanding in the grounds of Bowhill, Newark Castle is an impressive ruined tower of five storeys, rectangular in plan, dating from the 15th century. The lands were acquired by Archibald, Earl of Douglas, around 1423, but it was kept by the Crown after the downfall of the Black Douglases in 1455, and given to Margaret of Denmark, wife of James III, in 1473. The castle was besieged by the English in 1547 led by Lord Gray of Wilton, although apparently not captured, but then was burnt in 1548.

In 1645 one hundred followers of the Marquis of Montrose, mostly women, captured after the Battle of Philiphaugh, were shot, stabbed, slashed or bludgeoned to death in the barmkin of Newark. In 1810 large quantities of bones and skulls were dug up near the castle, at the field known as Slain Mens Lea. It is said that ghostly cries and screams of anguish can sometimes be heard at Newark.

The castle was altered for Anna, Duchess of Monmouth and Buccleuch, about 1690-1700. Her husband, James, Duke of Monmouth, was executed in 1685 for rebelling against James VII. Wordsworth visited the castle in 1831 with Sir Walter Scott. The ruin may be viewed from the exterior.

40 miles south of Edinburgh, 83 miles south-east of Glasgow, 3 miles west of Selkirk, south of A708, Bowhill (signposted).
NT 426278   OS: 73   TD7 5ET
Bowhill House: open for guided tours only: Jul, daily 13.00-15.30 (last tour), also Easter & some wknds in May & Aug - check with house; country estate open Apr-Sep, Wed-Mon 10.00-17.00, closed Tue. Venue

for weddings and events. Newark Castle is signposted from drive and there is limited parking at that castle.
Tel: 01750 22204   Web: www.bowhillhouse.co.uk
Features: Parking. Gift shop. Tea room. WC. Disabled access to courtyard and public rooms barring one. Gardens and grounds. Adventure playground. Admission charged.
Abbotsford (7 miles)
Traquair House (17 miles)
Floors Castle (21 miles)
Ferniehirst Castle (22 miles)
Mellerstain (22 miles)

Newark Castle

BRAEMAR CASTLE

Colour photos page C7

S et in a rugged and scenic part of Scotland, Braemar Castle is an altered L-plan tower house, dating from the 17th century. The building has a round stair-tower in the re-entrant angle, and bartizans crowning the corners. The tower is surrounded by 18th-century star-shaped artillery defences. There is an unventilated pit-prison, and the original iron yett.

The basement is vaulted, but much of the rest of the interior has been altered into a comfortable and charming residence.

The castle was built in 1628 by John Erskine, Earl of Mar. The Earls of Mar

Braemar Castle

supported William and Mary when the Stewart James VII was deposed in 1689. As a result the castle was captured and burnt out by John Farquharson of Inverey, the Black Colonel, who was a staunch Jacobite. It was left a ruin until 1748.

Although the family had resisted the Jacobites until then, John, 6th (or 11th) Earl of Mar, led the 1715 Jacobite Rising. He was more of a politician than a soldier, however, and the rebellion fizzled out. Mar fled abroad and was stripped of his lands. The property passed to the Farquharsons of Invercauld, and after the 1745-6 Jacobite Rising was taken over by the government, refurbished, and turned into a barracks, some of the walls bearing the scribblings of the garrison. The troops left in 1797, and castle was restored and reoccupied by the Farquharsons in the early 19th century. Queen Victoria visited when she attended the Braemar gathering.

Since 2007, the castle has been operated by the community of Braemar.

One story is that Braemar is haunted by the ghost of a young blonde-haired woman. A couple on their honeymoon were staying in the castle in the second half of the 19th century. Early in the morning the husband left to go hunting, but his young and inexperienced wife woke later and, not knowing about the hunting, believed she has been abandoned, having not pleased her husband in the marital bed. In despair, the poor woman threw herself from the battlements. Her ghost is said to haunt the castle, searching for her husband. It is thought that she only appears to those who have recently been married. Ghostly footsteps, the light tread of a woman, have also been reported.

Another spirit said to haunt the castle is that of John Farquharson of Inverey, mentioned above.

59 miles east of Aberdeen, 93 miles north of Edinburgh, 0.25 miles east of Braemar village, on A93, at Braemar Castle (signposted).
NO 156924 OS: 43 AB35 5XR
Open Easter-Oct – check with castle for days and times. Venue for weddings and events.
Tel: 01339 741219 Web: www.braemarcastle.co.uk
Features: Parking. Gift shop. Refreshments. WC. Disabled access limited to courtyard. Courtyard garden. Picnic area. Admission charged. The village of Braemar has many amenities.
Nearest:
Kildrummy Castle (35 miles)
Craigievar Castle (35 miles)
Crathes Castle (43 miles)
Ballindalloch Castle (45 miles)
Castle Fraser (46 miles)

BRODICK CASTLE

Colour photo page C5

Occupying a magnificent site overlooking Brodick Bay, Brodick Castle is a magnificent castle and mansion, and incorporates an old stronghold at one end, the lower part of which may date from the 13th century. The basement of the old part is vaulted, and contained the original kitchen. The castle was extended down the centuries and then in the mid 19th century was remodelled into a lavish stately home.

Arran was held by the Norsemen until driven out by Somerled in the 12th century, and the property only passed to the Scottish Crown in 1266. The Stewarts of Menteith built the original castle, but it was held by the English during the Wars of Independence until 1307 when it was recaptured by the Scots. The castle was damaged by English ships in 1406, and by the MacDonald Lord of the Isles about 1455.

Arran passed to the Hamiltons in 1503. James, 1st Hamilton Earl of Arran, rebuilt the castle about 1510, but it was damaged in a raid in 1528 between feuding Campbells and MacLeans, and again in 1544 by the Earl of Lennox for Henry VIII of England. The castle was captured by the Campbells in 1639, only to be retaken by the Hamiltons. In the 1650s the castle was occupied by Cromwell's troops.

Brodick Castle

Brodick Castle, Dining Room

Extensive additions were made in 1844 by the architect James Gillespie Graham for the marriage of Princess Marie of Baden to William, 11th Duke of Hamilton, and in 1958 Brodick was taken over by The National Trust for Scotland. There are fine gardens and grounds.

A Grey Lady is said to haunt the older part of the castle, her spirit possibly that of one of three women starved to death in the dungeons because they had plague.

50 miles west and south of Glasgow, 96 miles west and south of Edinburgh, 2.5 miles north of Brodick on Isle of Arran, off A841, at Brodick Castle (signposted).
NS 016378 OS: 69 KA27 8HY
NTS: Castle open Apr or Easter, daily 11.00-15.00; May-Sep, daily 11.00-16.00; Oct, daily for guided tours only 11.00-15.00; last entry 30 mins before closing; shop and tearoom same days; country park open all year, daily 9.00-sunset. Regular CalMac ferry from Ardrossan in Ayrshire on mainland to Brodick village; CalMac also runs a ferry from Lochranza on the north of Arran to Claonaig near Tarbert in Kintyre.
Tel: 0844 493 2152 Web: www.nts.org.uk
Features: Parking. Gift shop. Restaurant. WC. Gardens and country park. Adventure playground. Nature trail and access to Goatfell. Disabled WC and access. Admission charged.
Skipness Castle (30 miles (ferry))
Dean Castle (33 miles (ferry))
Rothesay Castle (42 miles (two ferries))
Newark Castle (43 miles (ferry))
Mount Stuart (44 miles (two ferries))

Brodie Castle

Colour photo page C8

A large and impressive building, Brodie Castle was mostly built in the 16th and 17th centuries, but may date in part from the 12th century, although this is disputed. The castle consists of a large Z-plan tower house, with extensive additions, which was further enlarged in the 19th century by the architect William Burn. The old tower rises to four storeys and a garret within a corbelled-out parapet. A wide stair-turret, with a conical roof, is corbelled out in the re-entrant angle.

The basement contains five vaulted chambers, including a kitchen with a great fireplace and bread oven. The only windows are slits and gunloops. The hall, on the first floor, is also vaulted, and there is an extensive library with some 6000 books, as well as other fine interiors.

The property was owned by the Brodies from 1160. The castle was burnt in 1645 by Lord Lewis Gordon, because the Brodies were Covenanters, although much of the internal work survived. It was damaged accidentally by fire in 1786. The house was renovated in 1980 after passing to The National Trust for Scotland.

Brodie Castle

Brodie Castle, Blue Sitting Room

The castle has a ghost story, possibly regarding Lady Margaret Duff, who was the wife of James Brodie, the then chief. In 1786 she fell asleep in front of the fire and her clothes were set alight and she burned to death. An apparition of a woman was reported in the nursery room in 1992.

The remains of a child were found when a turnpike stair was being renovated, and are on display in the Charter Room.

24 miles east and north of Inverness, 162 miles north of Edinburgh, 4 miles west of Forres, off A96, at Brodie Castle (signposted).
NH 980578   OS: 27   IV36 2TE
NTS: open Apr, daily 10.30-16.30; May-Jun and Sep-Oct, Sun-Thu 10.00-16.30; Jul-Aug, daily 10.30-17.00; last tour 60 mins before closing; grounds open all year, daily (car park fee); shop and tearoom also open on Sat, May-Jun & Sep-Oct.
Tel: 0844 493 2156   Web: www.nts.org.uk
Features: Parking. Gift shop. Tearoom. WC. Picnic area. Garden and adventure playground. Disabled facilities. Admission charged.
Cawdor Castle (11 miles)
Spynie Palace (18 miles)
Ballindalloch Castle (26 miles)
Balvenie Castle (32 miles)
Huntly Castle (44 miles)

CAERLAVEROCK CASTLE

Colour photo page C8

O nce a formidable fortress and still a magnificent ruin, Caerlaverock Castle has a unique triangular courtyard with a gatehouse at one corner, round towers at the others, and ranges of buildings between. The castle is still defended by a wet moat with ditches and embankments beyond the moat. An earlier moated castle, reduced to footings, stands nearby and can also be visited.

The gatehouse of Caerlaverock has two tall round towers, pierced by many gunloops, flanking the entrance, and was reached by a drawbridge over the moat. The gatehouse needed to be repaired and was given heavy machiolations in the late 15th century. The basement is vaulted, and a tall late 15th-century stair-tower has been added. A fine vaulted hall occupied the first floor.

One of the round towers, Murdoch's Tower – so called because Murdoch,

Caerlaverock Castle, gatehouse

Caerlaverock Castle, Nithsdale Lodging

Duke of Albany, was imprisoned here before his execution in 1425 – remains to its full height, but the other was demolished to foundations. The curtain wall, on this side, was also dismantled.

There were ranges of buildings on each side of the courtyard. Little remains of one side, but the other ranges survive to the wallhead. A fine Renaissance range, the Nithsdale Lodging, built in 1634, has two large chambers on the first floor over barrel-vaulted cellars. The windows are large and are crowned with elaborate carvings.

The castle was built in the 13th century by the Maxwells, and has a long eventful history. It was captured by the English in 1300, after a siege by Edward I of England, the event being commemorated in a poem in medieval French *Le Siege de Kalavreock*. The Scots fought bravely but were still all executed, according to one story. The castle was held by the English until 1312, when the keeper, Sir Eustace Maxwell, joined the Scots. He successfully resisted an English attack, but afterwards slighted the castle.

In the 1330s, the castle was repaired. Herbert Maxwell submitted to Edward III of England in 1347, and in 1357 Roger Kirkpatrick captured the castle for the Scots, although Kirkpatrick was later murdered here. There was further rebuilding in 1452-88 by Robert, 2nd Lord Maxwell. He added the machicolated parapets to the towers, and remodelled the gatehouse.

James V visited the castle prior to defeat at Solway Moss in 1542. The castle was surrendered to the English three years later, as part of the negotiated settlement, but was later recaptured by the Scots, only to be taken and slighted by an English force in 1570.

The Maxwells had a bitter feud with the Johnstones, and this came to battle in 1593 near Lockerbie when the Maxwells and their allies were routed and

Caerlaverock Castle

John Maxwell, 8th Lord, was slain. His son, the 9th Lord and another John, was executed in 1612 for murdering Sir James Johnstone, chief of the Johnstones. Robert Maxwell, 10th Lord, was made Earl of Nithsdale in 1620.

In 1640, the Earl and his garrison of 200 men surrendered the castle to a force of Covenanters after a siege of 13 weeks. Caerlaverock was then reduced by demolishing much of the curtain wall and one corner tower, and unroofing the rest. The Maxwells moved to Terregles, then to Traquair House.

By the late 18th century, the ruin was already popular with visitors, and the castle was transferred to the care of the State for consolidation in 1946.

84 miles south and east of Glasgow, 86 miles south and west of Edinburgh, 7 miles south and east of Dumfries, off B725, at Caerlaverock Castle (signposted).
NY 026656 OS: 84 DG1 4RU
Historic Scotland: open Apr-Sep, daily 9.30-17.30; Oct-Mar, daily 9.30-16.30; closed 25/26 Dec and 1/2 Jan; last entry 30 mins before closing. Cafe has restricted opening hours in winter.
Tel: 01387 770244 Web: www.historic-scotland.gov.uk
Features: Parking. Nature trail to older castle. Shop. Cafe. WC. Disabled access to shop, cafe and most of ground floor and courtyard of castle. Admission charged.
Drumlanrig Castle (26 miles)
Threave Castle (30 miles)
Cardoness Castle (39 miles)
Hermitage Castle (45 miles)
Dumfries House (53 miles)

CALLENDAR HOUSE

Colour photos page C9

Set in the picturesque and popular park, Callendar House is a large sprawling ornate mansion, rising to three storeys, with a profusion of towers and turrets. The mansion incorporates an old castle, which once had a deep ditch and courtyard, and still has very thick walls. There are extensive designed policies with woodland walks, a boating pond and a section of the Antonine Wall.

The property was held by the Livingstones from the 14th century. Mary, Queen of Scots, stayed here several times in the 1560s. The Livingstones were made Earls of Callendar in 1641, and then of Linlithgow, but the castle was stormed and captured by Cromwell in 1651. The Livingstones were forfeited for their part in the 1715 Jacobite Rising, and the house was leased to William Boyd, 4th Earl of Kilmarnock, although he was himself beheaded for his part in the 1745 Rising. Bonnie Prince Charlie had stayed here in 1745; and General Hawley and a Hanoverian army camped near here before going on to defeat at the nearby Battle of Falkirk the next year.

The house passed to William Forbes, a prosperous copper merchant, and he and his descendants remodelled and extended the house. It is now in the care of the local council and houses displays on the house and area, including

Callendar House

Callendar House

the 1825 Kitchen, The Story of Callendar House, and the Park Gallery with changing displays of contemporary visual art.

One story is that the house is haunted by the ghost of a young woman. During a wedding, a game of hide and seek was played. The girl hid in a trunk in the attic, but was then trapped and suffocated, not being found for three days.

24 miles east and north of Glasgow, 26 miles west of Edinburgh, to south of Falkirk, off A803, in Callendar Park, at Callendar House (signposted).
NS 898794   OS: 65   FK1 1YR
Open all year, Mon-Sat 10.00-17.00; also Apr-Sep, Sun 14.00-17.00; open most public hols; closed Xmas and New Year; park, open all year.
Tel: 01324 503770   Web: www.falkirkcommunitytrust.org/venues/
Features: Parking. Shop. Tearoom. WC. Disabled access. Displays, events and exhibitions. Park. Wedding and event venue.
Nearest:
Linlithgow Palace (8 miles)
Blackness Castle (13 miles)
The Binns (13 miles)
Stirling Castle (17 miles)
Hopetoun House (18 miles)

CARDONESS CASTLE

Colour photo page C10

Crowning a rocky mound above the Water of Fleet, Cardoness Castle is a late 15th-century, plain tower, rectangular in plan, of six storeys and formerly a garret within a flush parapet. Remains of (probably recreated) vaulted outbuildings survive in the ruined courtyard.

The entrance leads through a mural lobby to a guardroom and to a turnpike stair which climbs to the roof level. The basement is vaulted and consists of two rooms, and there is a pit-prison. The hall, on the first floor and formerly a grand apartment, has a wide moulded fireplace and fine carved cupboards. A straight stair, from the turnpike stair, leads to the second floor, which had two rooms, also with moulded fireplaces. There are good views from the top of the tower.

Cardoness Castle

The lands were held by the Cardoness family but, after most of them had reputedly drowned while out skating on a frozen loch, passed by marriage to the MacCullochs. This was in around 1450, and the MacCullochs built the castle.

They were an unruly and violent lot. James MacCulloch, 2nd laird, was outlawed in 1471 and again in 1480. His successor, Ninian, robbed his father's widow of all her goods and he may have been executed in 1509. Thomas MacCulloch, his son, besieged the Adairs of Dunskey in 1489, and soon after plundered the castle of his kinsman, MacCulloch of Adair. Thomas died at the Battle of Flodden in 1513. The property went to Alexander MacCulloch in 1516, and he raided the Isle of Man in the 1530s, commemorated by the Isle of Man verse: 'God keep the good corn, the sheep, and the bullock, From Satan, from sin, and from Cutlar M'Culloch'. He also dragged Marion Peebles, widow of the then Gordon owner of Cardoness, from her sick bed and left her on a dung heap, there to die.

The last of the family was Sir Godfrey MacCulloch, who shot William Gordon of Buck (or Bush) o' Bield in 1690, fled abroad, returned and was spotted in St Giles in Edinburgh. He was beheaded in 1697 by the Maiden, an early Scottish guillotine preserved in the National Museum of Scotland in Edinburgh, and is said by some to be the last person executed in this manner in Scotland.

Cardoness had passed because of debt to the Gordons in 1629, and then went to others. There are stories of a curse which afflicted the owners of Cardoness Castle, leading each family to eventual ruin, as well as stories of ghostly apparitions being seen in the tower.

98 miles south of Glasgow, 109 miles south-east of Edinburgh, 31 miles west and south of Dumfries, 0.75 miles south-west of Gatehouse of Fleet, off B796 north of junction with A75, at Cardoness Castle (signposted).
NX 591552   OS: 83   DG7 2EH
Historic Scotland: open Apr-Sep, daily 9.30-17.30.
Tel: 01557 814427   Web: www.historic-scotland.gov.uk
Features: Parking. Shop. WC. Picnic area. Limited disabled access. Admission charged.
Nearest:
Threave Castle (13 miles)
Caerlaverock Castle (39 miles)
Drumlanrig Castle (44 miles)
Culzean Castle (58 miles)
Dumfries House (63 miles)

CARNASSERIE CASTLE

Colour photo page C10

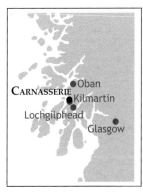

Brooding above the road running through the glen, Carnasserie Castle is a large ruined 16th-century tower house of five storeys and a garret, with an integral lower hall-block and second tower, which contains the entrance and a wide stair. The parapet has open rounds at three of the corners, and a corbelled-out bartizan at the other. The walls are pierced by many gunloops and shot-holes. A courtyard has an arch dated 1681.

The entrance, in one corner of the second tower, is surmounted by a Gaelic inscription urging faith in God. The entrance to the basement led, through a long narrow passage, to a wine-cellar, a kitchen with a fireplace and stone sink, and other cellars. The stone vaults of this block have gone.

The hall, on the first floor above, has an ornamental fireplace. Private chambers occupied the floors above, and the main bedchambers, one with a fine moulded fireplace on the first floor, were in the tower house.

There were gardens around the castle.

The property was held by the MacLachlans in 1436, then by the Campbell Earls of Argyll but was given in 1559 to John Carswell, who built the present castle. Carswell published the first ever book in Gaelic in 1567, the Gaelic

Carnasserie Castle

33

Carnasserie Castle

version of the *Book of Common Order*. He was Rector of Kilmartin, then Chancellor of the Chapel-Royal at Stirling. He was made Bishop of the Isles in 1566 by Mary, Queen of Scots and had a substantial income. On his death in 1572, he was buried at Ardchattan Priory, north of Oban, which stands on a lovely spot and may be visited.

The property passed to the Campbells of Auchenbreck in 1643. John Campbell of Ardkinglas, implicated in the murder of John Campbell of Cawdor in 1592 during a feud between different branches of the Campbells, was imprisoned and tortured in the castle until he confessed to the murder.

Carnasserie was captured and sacked by the MacLeans and MacLachlans during the Earl of Argyll's rebellion of 1685. The property was sold to the Malcolms of Poltalloch, and is now in the care of Historic Scotland.

97 miles west and north of Glasgow, 129 miles west of Edinburgh, 8.5 miles north of Lochgilphead, off A816, 2 miles north of village of Kilmartin, at Carnasserie Castle (signposted).
NM 837009   OS: 55   PA31 8RQ
Historic Scotland: Access at all reasonable times – short but steep walk up to the castle.
Web: www.historic-scotland.gov.uk
Features: Parking. Picnic area.
Nearest:
Skipness Castle (20 miles)
Dunstaffnage Castle (32 miles)
Inveraray Castle (33 miles)
Kilchurn Castle (34 miles)
Duart Castle, Mull (43 miles (ferry))

CASTLE CAMPBELL

Colour photo page C11

An impressive and picturesque building in a beautiful position, Castle Campbell was built where the Burns of Care and Sorrow join, overlooked by Gloom Hill, and was originally known as Castle Gloom. A large strong 15th-century tower, altered in later centuries and well preserved, stands at one corner of a substantial courtyard enclosed by a curtain wall.

The courtyard is entered by an arched pend, originally through a gatehouse. The tower rises four storeys to a parapet with open rounds at each corner. One entrance to the tower led to the vaulted basement and to a straight stair, in the thickness of the wall, to the first floor. The other entrance, at first-floor level, was reached by an external stair. The hall, on the first floor, is vaulted, and has a prison in the thickness of one wall, reached via a hatch in the stone floor.

A later range also contains a hall, and an arched loggia joins the lower storeys together.

The property passed by marriage to Colin Campbell, 1st Earl of Argyll and Chancellor of Scotland, and he had the name changed to Castle Campbell by an Act of Parliament in 1489. The 2nd Earl, Archibald, was killed at the Battle of Flodden in 1513, while the 4th Earl, another Archibald, took a prominent part in the defeat at the Battle of Pinkie in 1547 and in the siege of Haddington the following year. John Knox stayed at Castle Campbell in 1566.

The Marquis of Montrose defeated the 8th Earl and 1st Marquis of Argyll,

Castle Campbell

Castle Campbell

another Archibald, at the battles of Inverlochy and Kilsyth in 1645, but failed to capture the castle, although he ravaged the lands. The 8th Earl was responsible for hanging, drawing and quartering Montrose in 1651 – Argyll himself was later executed in 1661 after the Restoration. Cromwell's forces had occupied the castle in 1653, and only part was restored after being torched. The 9th Earl, yet another Archibald, was condemned to death for treason, escaped to start a rebellion, but was captured and executed in 1685.

George, 6th Duke of Argyll, sold the castle in the early 19th century, and in 1948 it was taken over by The National Trust for Scotland. There are fine walks up to the castle through Dollar Glen, which is open all year and in the care of the NTS.

39 miles north-east of Edinburgh, 36 miles north-east of Glasgow, 14 miles west of Stirling, 0.5 miles north of Dollar, off A91, in Dollar Glen, at Castle Campbell (signposted).
NS 962994 OS: 58 FK14 7PP
Historic Scotland: open all year: Apr-Sep, daily 9.30-18.30; Oct-Mar, Sat-Wed 9.30-16.30, closed Thu & Fri; last ticket 30 mins before closing; closed 25/26 Dec and 1/2 Jan.
Tel: 01259 742408 Web: www.historic-scotland.gov.uk
Features: Parking. Gift shop. Refreshments. WC. Limited disabled access. Admission charged.
Nearest:
Lochleven Castle (13 miles)
Stirling Castle (14 miles)
Culross Palace (14 miles)
Doune Castle (19 miles)
Drummond Castle Gardens (23 miles)

CASTLE FRASER

Colour photo page C11

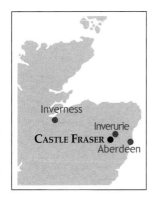

Impressive and well preserved, Castle Fraser is a tall and massive Z-plan tower house, mostly dating from between 1575 and 1636. There is a large main block, a square tower at one corner, and a great round tower at the opposite corner. Two projecting wings form a courtyard, the final side being completed by other buildings, one with an arched gateway. The castle was built by the mason John Bell.

The oldest part is a plain 15th-century tower of four storeys and an attic. The great round tower rises two storeys higher to finish in a flat roof. The corners of the main block and square tower are crowned by two-storey corbelled-out bartizans with shot-holes. The upper storeys of the main block and both towers project on corbelling and have dormer windows. The walls are pierced with many gunloops, slits and shot-holes.

Over the present entrance are panels dated 1576, 1683, and 1795.

The original entrance, in the re-entrant angle with the square tower, leads to the vaulted basement, containing a kitchen and cellars. It also leads to a wide turnpike stair, climbing to the first-floor hall. The interior was remodelled

Castle Fraser

in 1838, and there are many Fraser family portraits, as well as a Laird's Lug and secret stairs.

The property was acquired by the Frasers in 1454, and in 1633 the family was created Lord Fraser. The Frasers were Covenanters, and their lands were ravaged in 1638, and then in 1644 by the Marquis of Montrose. Later the Frasers were Jacobites, and Charles, 4th Lord, died a fugitive, falling from a cliff the year after the 1715 Jacobite Rising.

In 1976 the property was donated to The National Trust for Scotland.

There is an 18th-century walled garden, and a grassed ampitheatre, lake and woodland.

One story associated with the castle is that a young woman was murdered in the Green Room of the castle's Round Tower – either in the 19th century or the distant past, depending on the version of the tale – and that her body was dragged down stairs before being buried. It was said that blood from her corpse, which stained the stairs and the hearth of the chamber, could not be cleaned off, and the stairs were eventually boarded over to hide the stains.

139 miles north and east of Edinburgh, 16 miles west of Aberdeen, 6.5 miles south-west of Inverurie, off B977, 3 miles south of Kemnay, at Castle Fraser (signposted).
NJ 724126 OS: 38 AB51 7LD
NTS: open Apr-Jun & Sep-Oct, Wed-Sun 12.00-17.00; Jul-Aug, daily 11.00-17.00; also open Bank Hol mons in summer; last entry 45 mins before closing; grounds and gardens open all year.
Tel: 0844 493 2164 Web: www.nts.org.uk
Features: Parking. Gift shop. Tea room. Picnic area. Garden and grounds. Walled garden. Waymarked walks. Disabled access to ground floor of castle. Adventure playground. Admission charged.
Nearest:
Drum Castle (13 miles)
Crathes Castle (13 miles)
Craigievar Castle (14 miles)
Tolquhon Castle (21 miles)
Haddo House (21 miles)

CASTLE MENZIES

Colour photos page C12

A grand and substantial building in a picturesque location, Castle Menzies (pronounced 'Mingiz') is an altered and extended 16th-century tower house. The castle has a large main block of three storeys and an attic, with two square towers of five storeys, projecting at opposite corners, making it Z-plan. Round bartizans crown corners of the building, and the walls are pierced by many shot holes. There was an extension in the 18th century, which involved the remodelling of the building with a new grand stair. A large baronial wing was added in 1840, designed by the architect William Burn. The 18th-century extension was demolished because of problems with damp.

The castle stood in landscaped grounds, with many specimen trees, but this has mostly gone, although the walled garden is being restored.

The basement of the castle is vaulted, and the grand hall is on the first floor. A wide turnpike stair in one tower leads to all floors, and the original entrance has an iron yett. There is some fine wooden panelling, as well as old plaster ceilings. There are many rooms in the towers and the floors above.

This was a property of the Menzies family. Their original castle was at Comrie, but this was burnt in 1487 and Sir Robert Menzies built a new stronghold, called the Place of Weem, near or at the site of the present castle. In 1502 this building in turn was burned by Neil Stewart of Garth, who

Castle Menzies

imprisoned Robert Menzies in the dungeon at Garth, until he signed away some of his lands. Stewart was convinced that the lands were his as part of a dowry settlement, but the case was found against him and he was forced to make restitution. The Menzies clan fought against the Marquis of Montrose, and Alexander the then chief, although 80 years of age, died after a skirmish, while his son, another Alexander, was slain at the Battle of Inverlochy in 1645.

The castle was occupied by Cromwell's forces, under General Monck, in the 1650s, but the family were made baronets of Nova Scotia in 1665. The chiefs did not support the Jacobite Risings, and the castle was captured and occupied by Jacobites in 1715. Bonnie Prince Charlie stayed here for two nights in 1746, but four days later the castle was taken by Hanoverian forces, led by the Duke of Cumberland. The chiefs again did not support the Rising, but many of the clan, including their leader Archibald Menzies of Shian, were killed at Culloden in 1746.

The clan chiefs moved to nearby Farleyer and the castle was rented out, including by Maharajah Duleep Singh, who stayed in 1857-8. The last of the Menzies line died in 1918, and between 1939 and 1945 the castle was used as a Polish Army medical supplies depot.

The castle became derelict, but has been being restored by a trust established by the Clan Menzies Society, who acquired the building in 1957. A museum about the Menzies clan has exhibits including Bonnie Prince Charlie's death mask, the bed he slept in at the castle, and information on the influential botanist and explorer, Archibald Menzies.

The Menzies family were buried at the nearby Old Kirk of Weem, and in that building are memorials to the chiefs, dating from the 16th century. The kirk is also in the care of the Menzies Heritable Trust and may be visited by arrangement.

Aberfeldy is a pleasant village with places to eat and shop, and nearby is the Birks of Aberfeldy, a lovely and popular (but in places very steep) walk up through the gorge (and back) of the Moness Burn.

---

76 miles north of Edinburgh, 21 miles north and west of Perth, 1.5 miles west and north of Aberfeldy, just north of B846, at Castle Menzies (signposted).
NN 837496   OS: 52   PH15 2JD
Open Apr or Easter-Oct, Mon-Sat 10.30-17.00, Sun 14.00-17.00; last entry 30 mins before closing. Venue for weddings and other occasions. Tel: 01887 820982   Web: www.castlemenzies.org
Facilities: Parking. Gift shop. Tea room (no lunches: House of Menzies or Aberfeldy are close by). WC. Limited disabled access. Walled garden. Exhibitions. Admission charged.
Nearest:
Blair Castle (23 miles)
Drummond Castle Gardens (29 miles;)
Huntingtower (32 miles)
Scone Palace (34 miles)
Glamis Castle (45 miles)

CASTLE OF MEY

Colour photo page C13

CASTLE OF MEY
Thurso
Wick
Inverness

The most northerly inhabited castle of the British mainland, Castle of Mey is an impressive Z-plan tower house, which dates from the 16th century. The castle has a main block of three storeys and an attic, with four-storey square towers, one a stair-tower, at opposite corners. Corbelled-out turrets crown some corners, and the walls are pierced by gunloops. The building was extended and altered in the 18th century, then in 1819 by the architect William Burn, and again in 1957.

There is an attractive walled garden.

The basement is vaulted and houses the original kitchen with a large fireplace and other cellars. The hall was on the first floor.

Castle of Mey

41

Castle of Mey, garden

The lands originally belonged to the Bishop of Caithness, but in 1566 were acquired by the Sinclair Earls of Caithness, who built the castle. George, 6th Earl, bankrupted the family, and the earldom was claimed by the Campbells of Breadalbane, although this was disputed by Sinclair of Keiss. The Sinclairs eventually recovered the earldom and castle, although not without much bloodshed after the Campbells had led a bloody campaign in Caithness.

Neil MacLeod of Assynt, who betrayed the Marquis of Montrose, was imprisoned in the castle.

In 1952 the property was sold to Her Majesty Queen Elizabeth the Queen Mother, who had it restored. She used the castle every summer until her death in 2002, and the property then went to The Castle of Mey Trust.

276 miles north of Edinburgh, 123 miles north and east of Inverness, 14 miles east of Thurso, 21 miles north of Wick, off A836, at Castle of Mey (signposted).
ND 290739 OS: 12 KW14 8XH
House open early May-Sep, daily 10.20-last admission 16.00; shop and tea room same days but open until 17.00.
Tel: 01847 851473 Web: www.castleofmey.org.uk
Features: Parking. Shop. Tea room. WC. Disabled access restricted to principal floor. Animal centre. Walled garden. Admission charged.
Nearest:
Dunrobin Castle (71 miles)
Cawdor Castle (134 miles)
Brodie Castle (144 miles)
Spynie Palace (161 miles)
Ballindalloch Castle (168 miles)

CAWDOR CASTLE

Colour photo page C13

A magnificent and largely unaltered stronghold, Cawdor Castle has a tall, plain but imposing tower, dating from the 14th century; the parapet and turrets were added in 1454. The castle has a deep ditch, and is reached by a drawbridge. Mainly three-storey ranges, gabled and crowned with bartizans and corbelled-out chambers, were built on all sides of the keep in the 16th and 17th centuries. There is a pit prison.

Across the drawbridge defending the entrance is a massive iron yett, which

Cawdor Castle

Cawdor Castle

was brought here from Lochindorb Castle after 1455. The tower has very thick walls pierced by small windows. Both the basement and the third floor are vaulted. In a later range is an iron yett and postern gate to the moat and some fine 17th-century fireplaces, and there are many portraits, fine furnishings and a collection of tapestries.

The castle stands in many acres of wooded grounds and has three gardens: a walled garden, the colourful flower garden, and a wild garden.

The title Thane of Cawdor is associated with Macbeth, but King Duncan was not murdered here. The castle is not nearly old enough and, anyway, he was killed in battle near Spynie.

Donald, 1st Thane of Cawdor, took the name of Calder when granted the lands by Alexander II in 1236, although one story is that the family were descended from a brother of Macbeth. William, 3rd Thane, was murdered by Sir Alexander Rait of nearby Rait Castle. Donald, 5th Thane, built much of the present castle.

It was not decided where the site of the castle should be, so a donkey was allowed to rove at will until it came to a suitable spot by a tree. Cawdor was built over the tree, the trunk of which is in the vaulted basement. This was long believed to be a hawthorn, but in fact it proved to be a holly tree and it died in about 1372 – when the castle was built.

The Campbells obtained Cawdor by kidnapping the girl heiress, Muriel Calder, and marrying her in 1511, at the age of 12, to the Earl of Argyll's son, Sir John Campbell. Campbell of Inverliver led the kidnapping, and lost all six of his sons.

The Campbells of Cawdor, her descendants, remained at the castle.

Lachlan Cattanach, 11th Chief of the Macleans, became so unhappy with Catherine Campbell, his wife, that he had the poor woman chained to a rock in the Firth of Lorn to be drowned at high tide. However, she was rescued and taken to her father, Archibald Campbell, 2nd Earl of Argyll. As a result, Maclean was murdered in his bed in Edinburgh by Sir John Campbell of Cawdor, the lady's brother, in 1523.

John Campbell of Cawdor was murdered at Knipoch in 1592, having been shot three or four times as he sat by the fire, during a feud between different branches of the Campbells. John Campbell of Ardkinglas was implicated and was imprisoned and tortured in Carnasserie Castle until he confessed to the murder.

The Campbells of Cawdor gave refuge to Simon Fraser, Lord Lovat, during his flight from Hanoverian troops in 1746 during the Jacobite Rising, and hid him in a secret room in the roof. Fraser was eventually caught and executed. Bonnie Prince Charlie had visited the same year.

The family were made Barons Cawdor in 1796 and then Earls Cawdor in 1827, and they still own the castle.

A ghost clad in a blue velvet dress has reputedly been seen here, as has an apparition of John Campbell 1st Lord Cawdor.

161 miles north of Edinburgh, 15 miles east and north of Inverness, 6 miles south-west of Nairn, on B9090 off A96, at Cawdor Castle (signposted).
NH 847499 OS: 27 IV12 5RD
Open May-early Oct, daily 10.00-17.00; last entry 30 mins before closing; opening outwith these times for groups by arrangement. Holiday accommodation. Venue for weddings and events.
Tel: 01667 404401 Web: www.cawdorcastle.com
Features: Parking. Gift shops. Licensed restaurant and snack bar. Gardens, grounds and nature trails. Golf course and putting. Disabled access to grounds; some of castle. Admission charged. Salmon fishing.
Nearest:
Brodie Castle (11 miles)
Spynie Palace (28 miles)
Ballindalloch Castle (40 miles)
Balvenie Castle (42 miles)
Huntly Castle (54 miles)

CRAIGIEVAR CASTLE

Colour photos page C14

A largely unaltered and very picturesque castle located among rolling hills, Craigievar Castle is a massive L-plan tower house of seven storeys, which was completed in 1626. Turrets, gables, chimney-stacks and corbelling crown the upper storeys, in contrast to the lower storeys, which are completely plain. The walls are rounded at the corners, and are harled and pink-washed. The square tower, in the re-entrant angle, is crowned by a balustraded parapet enclosing a flat roof, with a caphouse topped by an ogee roof. The castle stood in a small courtyard, with round towers at the corners, only one of which survives.

The entrance leads to a vestibule to three vaulted chambers, and to a straight stair in the centre of the house, which rises only to the first floor. The hall, with a private chamber, occupies the first floor, and is a magnificent vaulted apartment, with mixed groin- and barrel-vaulting and a fine plaster ceiling. A narrow stair leads down to the wine-cellar, and there is a small minstrels' gallery. The hall has a large fireplace with ornamental stone carving, and there is a

Craigievar Castle

Craigievar Castle

laird's lug, accessed from a narrow entrance in the adjoining passageway.

The floors above are occupied by many private chambers, reached by five turret stairs. Many of these rooms are panelled, and there is also good contemporary plasterwork.

The property belonged to the Mortimer family from 1457 or earlier, and they held it until 1610. They began the castle, but ran out of money, and it was sold to the Forbeses of Menie, who finished the building in 1626. William Forbes, a zealous Covenanter, was responsible for the 'putting down' of Gilderoy the freebooter and his band, and having them hanged in Edinburgh. He commanded a troop of horse in the Civil War, and was Sheriff of Aberdeen. Forbes of Brux and Paton of Grandhome, who were both Jacobites, hid in the laird's lug to avoid capture. The castle was taken over by The National Trust for Scotland in 1963.

Craigievar is said to be haunted by a Gordon, who was murdered by being pushed from one of the windows of the Blue Room by Sir John Forbes – although it appears this window formerly had bars. Another ghost is said to be a fiddler, drowned in a well in the kitchen, who only appears to members of the Forbes family.

Craigievar Castle, the Blue Room

126 miles north of Edinburgh, 28 miles west of Aberdeen, 6 miles south and west of Alford, off A980 1.5 miles north of junction with B9119, at Craigievar Castle (signposted).

NJ 566095   OS: 37   AB33 8JF

NTS: Castle open for guided tours Apr-Jun & Sep, Fri-Tue 11.00-16.45 (last entry); Jul & Aug, daily 11.00-16.45 (last entry); number on tours are limited so there may be wait until next available tour; groups of more than six people should book in advance; grounds, open all year. Tel: 0844 493 2174   Web: www.nts.org.uk

Features: Parking. Guided tours only. Shop. Picnic area. Admission charged. Venue for weddings and events.

Nearest:

Castle Fraser (14 miles)
Kildrummy Castle (14 miles)
Crathes Castle (18 miles)
Drum Castle (22 miles)
Tolquhon Castle (32 miles)

CRAIGMILLAR CASTLE

Colour photo page C15

Glasgow Edinburgh
CRAIGMILLAR

With magnificent views over the surrounding area, Craigmillar is a strong, imposing, extensive and very well-preserved ruin with a warren of chambers, corridors and stairs. The castle has a 14th-century L-plan tower, surrounded by a 15th-century heavily machicolated curtain wall with round corner towers and an intact wall-walk. The walls are pierced by inverted keyhole gunloops. Early in the 16th century the castle was given an additional walled courtyard, protected by a ditch.

The main L-plan tower is roofed with stone slabs, inside a parapet, and the stair is topped by a caphouse. The entrance is through a wide-arched entrance, and leads to a vaulted lobby and to a turnpike stair. The basement is vaulted and had an entresol floor. The large hall, on the first floor (second floor of the external ranges), has a fine hooded moulded fireplace and also had a mezzanine. The vaulted chamber in the wing was once the kitchen, and is reputed to be where Mary, Queen of Scots, stayed when she visited the castle. Another turnpike stair leads to battlements.

The courtyard enclosed three-storey ranges, with vaulted basements, which contained a kitchen and a long gallery, as well as many other chambers.

Craigmillar Castle

Craigmillar Castle, courtyard

The Prestons held the property from 1374, and built a new castle on the site of a much older stronghold – the property was once known as Gorton or Gourtoun. The Preston Aisle of St Giles Cathedral in Edinburgh was built in memory of Sir William Preston of Gorton, after he had given the church a reliquary containing the arm bone of St Giles which he had acquired in France.

The former fish pond, which can be seen in the field below the castle, is shaped into a P for the Preston family, and there are several heraldic panels with the Preston coat of arms.

In 1477 James III imprisoned his brother John, Earl of Mar, in one of its cellars, where he died, and James V visited the castle to escape 'the pest' in Edinburgh. The Earl of Hertford and the English burnt the castle in 1544, after valuables from Edinburgh had been stolen, although the damage done cannot have been extensive and the castle may have been taken without too much resistance from Sir Simon Preston, Provost of Edinburgh. Mary, Queen of Scots, visited Craigmillar often, and fled here in 1566 after the murder of Rizzio. It was at Craigmillar that Moray, Bothwell, and William Maitland of Lethington plotted Darnley's murder. James VI stayed in 1589.

In 1660 Sir John Gilmour, who was later President of the College of Justice, bought Craigmillar, and had the castle altered into a comfortable residence and reconstructed the range on the west side of the courtyard.

A walled-up skeleton, standing upright, was reportedly found in one of the vaults in 1813.

One story is that the unexplained smell of lavender has been repeatedly noticed in the great hall and that this is evidence of some supernatural activity. There are also stories of a Green Lady haunting the vicinity, said by some to be the one of the many ghosts of Mary, Queen of Scots.

4 miles south-east of Edinburgh Castle, on road between A6095 and
A68, just south of Craigmillar housing estate, at Craigmillar Castle
(signposted).
NT 288709   OS: 66   EH16 4SY
Historic Scotland: open all year: Apr-Sep, daily 9.30-17.30; Oct-Mar,
Sat-Wed 9.30-16.30; closed 25/26 Dec and 1/2 Jan; last entry 30 mins
before closing. 200 yard walk to property.
Tel: 0131 661 4445   Web: www.historic-scotland.gov.uk
Features: Parking. Shop. Refreshments. WC. Limited disabled access.
Admission charged.
Nearest:
Newhailes (3 miles)
Edinburgh Castle (4 miles)
Palace of Holyroodhouse (4 miles)
Lauriston Castle (8 miles)
Crichton Castle (10 miles)

Craigmillar Castle, Great Hall

CRAIGNETHAN CASTLE

Colour photo page C15

Standing on a promontory above a deep ravine in a pretty location, Craignethan is an early castle built to withstand artillery. A strong but comfortable tower was surrounded by a curtain wall on three sides, with a rampart protecting the landward side. There was also an outer courtyard.

The ruined but well-preserved main tower is squat and rectangular, with a corbelled-out parapet, open rounds at the corners, and a machiolation over the entrance. The entrance leads, through a large lobby on the first floor, to the hall and to a turnpike stair by the guardroom. The kitchen is also on the first floor, and the basement is vaulted and contained cellars.

There were large flanking towers, only one of which survives, and a massively thick rampart defending the main tower, which has been completely demolished. In the ditch, before the rampart, is a caponier, rediscovered in 1962 when the ditch was excavated: it must have been airless if ever used. The ditch was crossed by a drawbridge, which led to the gatehouse.

The property originally belonged to the Black Douglases, but passed to the Hamiltons in 1455. Sir James Hamilton of Finnart, a talented architect and the King's Superintendent of Palaces, built most of the castle in the 1530s. Hamilton, the illegitimate son of James Hamilton, Earl of Arran, was beheaded

Craignethan Castle

Craignethan Castle, window of tower

for treason in 1540, after a missile was fired at James V in Linlithgow, although his son eventually inherited his lands. Mary, Queen of Scots, is said to have spent the night here before Langside in 1568, although this is not certain. The Hamiltons certainly formed the main part of her army, but were defeated by the Earl of Moray and Mary fled to England. The garrison of Craignethan surrendered after the battle, but the castle was retaken by the Hamiltons, was attacked in 1579, then given up without a siege. Much of the defences were then demolished. Sir Walter Scott featured Craignethan in *Old Mortality*, but called it Tillietudlem.

The castle is said to be haunted by a headless ghost, perhaps the spirit of Mary, Queen of Scots, as well as other apparitions and manifestations.

23 miles south-east of Glasgow, 40 miles west and south of Edinburgh, 6.5 miles west and north of Lanark, off A72 at Crossford, at Craignethan Castle (signposted).
NS 816464   OS: 72   ML11 9PL
Historic Scotland: open Apr-Sep, daily 9.30-17.30; last ticket sold 30 mins before closing.
Tel: 01555 860364   Web: www.historic-scotland.gov.uk
Features: Parking. Shop. WC. Disabled access to courtyard. Picnic area. Admission charged.
Nearest:
Bothwell Castle (18 miles)
Pollok House (27 miles)
Dumfries House (33 miles)
Dean Castle (40 miles)
Linlithgow Palace (41 miles)

CRATHES CASTLE

Colour photos page C16

One of the finest castles in Scotland, Crathes is a massive 16th-century tower house of four storeys and an attic, square in plan, but with a small projecting wing, to which later work has been added. The upper storeys are adorned with much corbelling, bartizans, stair-turrets and decoration, while the lower storeys are very plain, apart from a large later window at first-floor level. There is a large and colourful walled garden with many unusual plants, and topiary and yew hedges. The 595 acres of grounds have waymarked trails.

The basement of the tower is vaulted, and contained the old kitchen and cellars, the wine-cellar having a small stair to the hall above. The castle still has an iron yett. The hall is vaulted, and there is a 16th-century Italian fireplace. There are many fine painted ceilings, and the top floor contains a long gallery.

Crathes Castle

54

Crathes Castle

The property was owned by the Burnetts of Leys from the 14th century, their original castle being in the now drained Loch of Leys. The jewelled ivory Horn of Leys is kept at Crathes, and was given to the Burnetts in 1323 by Robert the Bruce. Around 1553, the family began to build the new castle, but it was not completed until 1596.

One of the chambers, the Green Lady's room has a fine painted ceiling, but is said to be haunted. The ghost reportedly first appeared in the 18th century, and is seen crossing the chamber, with a baby in her arms, to disappear at the fireplace. The young woman seems to have been a daughter of the then laird, and had been dallying with a servant. Skeletons of a young woman and baby – or just the infant itself – were reportedly found by workmen under the hearthstone during renovations in the 19th century. The spectre is said to have been witnessed many times, once being described as appearing as a luminous block of ice.

Crathes Castle, the Long Gallery

125 miles north and east of Edinburgh, 18 miles west and south of Aberdeen, 3 miles east of Banchory, off A93, at Crathes Castle (signposted).

NO 734968   OS: 45   AB31 3QJ

NTS: Open Apr-Oct, daily 10.30-16.45; Nov-Dec, Sat & Sun only 10.30-15.45 (check winter opening); last admission 45 mins before closing; cafe and shop, Apr-Oct, daily; Nov-Dec, Tue-Sun (check winter opening); Garden and grounds, open all year, 9.00-sunset. Weddings and corporate events.

Tel: 0844 493 2166   Web: www.nts.org.uk

Features: Parking. Gift shop. Restaurant. Gardens, grounds and adventure playground. Plant sales. Disabled facilities, including access to ground floor and WC. Admission charged.

Nearest:

Drum Castle (6 miles)

Castle Fraser (13 miles)

Dunnottar Castle (16 miles)

Craigievar Castle (19 miles)

Edzell Castle (27 miles)

CRICHTON CASTLE

Colour photo page C17

A complex, large and imposing pile, Crichton Castle consists of ranges of buildings from the 14th to 16th centuries, enclosing a small courtyard. The castle stands in a valley in an attractive peaceful location above the River Tyne, and a unique feature of particular note is the diamond-faced facade of one block in the courtyard.

The oldest part is a 14th-century tower, formerly of three storeys, although quite ruinous. The basement was vaulted and had a pit-prison.

In the 15th century a new gatehouse of three storeys was added, then further ranges enclosing the courtyard. Another block was added in the 16th century, Italian Renaissance in style, with a magnificent arcaded, diamond-faced facade, based on a palace in Italy and unique in Scotland.

Outside the castle are the imposing roofless stables, which are said to be haunted by the ghost of Sir William Crichton.

The castle was a property of the Crichtons, and probably first built about 1370. Sir William Crichton, Chancellor of Scotland, entertained William, the young 6th Earl of Douglas, and his brother, David, before having them murdered at the Black Dinner in Edinburgh Castle in 1440. John Forrester slighted Crichton Castle in retaliation.

Sir William Crichton, however, founded the nearby Crichton Collegiate Church, where priests were to pray for his salvation. This is a substantial and

Crichton Castle

57

Crichton Castle, diamond-faced facade in courtyard

impressive edifice, dedicated to St Mary and St Kentigern, dating from 1449, with a square crenellated tower.

The Crichtons were forfeited for treason in 1488, and the property later passed to Patrick Hepburn, Lord Hailes, who was made Earl of Bothwell. One of the family was James Hepburn, 4th Earl, third husband of Mary, Queen of Scots. In 1559 the castle was besieged and captured by the Earl of Arran after Bothwell had seized some 4000 crowns from Elizabeth I, which had been meant for the Protestant cause. Mary, Queen of Scots, attended a wedding at Crichton Castle in 1562.

After Bothwell was forfeited in 1581 and imprisoned in Denmark, Crichton was given to Francis Stewart, who added the Renaissance range in the 1580s and remodelled the castle. Francis Stewart was, himself, such a wild and unruly fellow that in 1593 he was also forfeited.

Crichton does not appear to have been much used following this and

Crichton Collegiate Church

deteriorated into a romantic ruin. Turner painting the castle, while Sir Walter Scott included it in *Marmion*.

The castle is said to be haunted by a horseman who enters the castle by the original gate, which is now walled up.

15 miles south-east of Edinburgh, 3 miles south-west of Pathhead, 3 miles east of Gorebridge, off B6367, 0.5 miles south-west of Crichton village, at Crichton Castle (signposted).
NT 380612   OS: 66   EH37 5XA (car park)
Historic Scotland: Castle open Apr-Sep, daily 9.30-17.30; last admission 30 mins before closing.
Tel: 01875 320017   Wed: www.historic-scotland.gov.uk
Features: Parking (walk to castle 600 yards). Sales area. Admission charged.
Collegiate church open May-Sep, Sun 14.00-17.00
Tel: 01875 320502/364   Web: www.crichtonchurch.com
Nearest:
Craigmillar Castle (10 miles)
Newhailes (11 miles)
Palace of Holyroodhouse (14 miles)
Edinburgh Castle (15 miles)
Thirlestane Castle (16 miles)

CULROSS PALACE

Colour photo page C17

Set in the picturesque village by the banks of the Forth, Culross Palace, although built between 1597 and 1611, does not apparently have any fortified features, although one range is vaulted and the basement is lit by slits. The name 'palace' does not suggest any royal connection, but means residential accommodation, as opposed to a castle or fortified house. The complex consists of ranges of gabled yellow-washed buildings, with fabulous decorative paint work and original interiors. There is an unusual steeply terraced garden.

The palace was built for Sir George Bruce of Carnock, who made a fortune from coal mining, and developed mines that ran out, following seams of coal, underneath the Firth of Forth. Bruce took James VI into the tunnels and then out under the sea to Preston Island, an artificial island. The king was somewhat perturbed coming up in the middle of the water, until he was rowed back to the shore. A great storm devastated the Forth in March 1625 and flooded the coal workings, so that they could not be used again.

Bruce died in 1625 a few weeks after the disaster, and was buried in the parish church, where his elaborate and remarkable tomb is marked by his stone effigy and by that of his wife Margaret Primrose, as well as the kneeling statues of eight of his children.

Culross Palace

The palace passed in about 1700 to the Erskines, and the building has been carefully restored by The National Trust for Scotland.

The palace was a location for the movie *The Little Vampire* (2000), the BBC version of *The 39 Steps*, and the films *A Dying Breed* and *Captain America: The First Avenger*. The village of Culross is said to be haunted by a ghostly piper, sent off to search an underground passage, while there are also stories that the palace is haunted.

The NTS has a visitor centre and exhibition in the Town House of 1626, and the house of 1610, called The Study, is also open to visitors. Many other 16th- and 17th-century houses survive in the narrow streets of this ancient royal burgh, and can be viewed from outside. The ruins of Culross Abbey may also be visited, as can the parish church, which was remodelled from the nave of the abbey church.

Culross Abbey was a Cistercian establishment, dedicated to St Serf and St Mary. It was founded in 1217 by Malcolm, Earl of Fife, on the site of a Celtic Christian establishment. The abbey was dissolved at the Reformation and most of the buildings are ruinous, except the monk's choir, which has been used as the parish church since 1633.

In 1589 the lands of the abbey were given to the Colvilles of Culross, and Sir James Colville of Easter Wemyss was made Baron Colville of Culross in 1604. Near the abbey is Culross Abbey House, which dates from 1608 and was built for Edward Bruce, Lord Kinloss. It was formerly an impressive building, but was ruinous by about 1800. It was altered in 1830, and again in 1955 when much reduced in size.

23 miles west of Edinburgh, 31 miles east and north of Glasgow, 18 miles east of Stirling, in village of Culross, off B9037, at Culross Palace (signposted).

NS 986862 OS: 65 KY12 8JH

NTS: Palace, Study and Town House, open Apr-May, Thu-Mon 12.00-17.00; Jun-Aug, daily 12.00-17.00; Sep, Thu-Mon 12.00-17.00; Oct, Thu-Mon 12.000-17.00; palace garden, open all year; study and town house guided tours from palace only. Venue for weddings and events.

Tel: 0844 493 2189 Web: www.nts.org.uk

Features: Parking nearby. Shop. Tea room. WC. Garden. Disabled access to tea room and WC only. Admission charged.

Culross Abbey Church open summer, 10.00-dusk, winter 10.00-16.00

Nearest:

Castle Campbell (14 miles)

Aberdour Castle (14 miles)

Hopetoun House (17 miles)

Stirling Castle (18 miles)

The Binns (19 miles)

CULZEAN CASTLE

Colour photos page C18

Pronounced 'Cul-lane', Culzean Castle, a magnificent castellated mansion built between 1777–92, incorporates part of a 16th century L-plan tower house, which itself was built on the site of an older castle. The magnificent castle stands in a lovely spot in hundreds of acres of grounds, parkland and woodland by the shore of the Firth of Clyde, and there is a walled garden and woodland walks.

Culzean was a property of the Kennedys from the 12th century, and they may have had a stronghold here from then. Thomas Kennedy of Culzean was murdered by Gilbert Mure of Auchendrane in the course of a feud after the slaying of Gilbert Kennedy of Bargany in 1601. The castle was completely rebuilt, although it incorporates much of the old building, for the 9th and 10th Earls of Cassillis by the architect Robert Adam.

The property passed to The National Trust for Scotland in 1945. A flat within the building was reserved for use by President Dwight Eisenhower for his services to Britain during World War II and is now a luxury hotel. The elegant interior of Culzean includes the spectacular oval staircase and the circular saloon.

A ghostly piper is said to herald when one of the Kennedys is about to get

Culzean Castle

Culzean Castle, Circular Saloon

married, and to be heard playing on stormy nights. His apparition has reportedly been seen in the grounds. There are reputedly two others ghosts who haunt the castle, one a young woman dressed in a ball gown. There are also stories of a White Lady, said to be the ghost of a mistreated servant.

The castle was a location in the Edward Woodward film *The Wickerman*.

95 miles south-west of Edinburgh, 49 miles south and west of Glasgow, 13 miles south-west of Ayr, 5 miles west of Maybole, off A719, at Culzean Castle (signposted).
NS 233103   OS: 70   KA19 8LE
NTS: Castle open Apr-Oct, daily 10.30-17.00, last entry 16.00; visitor centre open Apr-Oct, daily 10.00-17.00; Nov-late Dec, Sat-Sun only 11.00-16.00; country park open all year, daily 9.30-sunset. Venue for weddings and events.
Tel: 0844 493 2149
Web: www.nts.org.uk / www.culzeanexperience.org
Features: Parking. Gift shops. Two cafes. WC. Picnic areas. Woodland walks. Gardens and adventure playground. Country park and visitor centre. Admission charged.
Nearest:
Dumfries House (24 miles)
Dean Castle (28 miles)
Pollok House (46 miles)
Drumlanrig Castle (50 miles)
Brodick Castle, Arran (52 miles (ferry))

DEAN CASTLE

Colour photo page C20

Glasgow Edinburgh

●**DEAN**
Kilmarnock

Interesting and imposing, Dean Castle has a 15th-century tower of three storeys and a garret with a flush crenellated parapet. Near the old tower is a palace block and a square tower, which has a corbelled-out parapet and corbiestepped gables. The tower and palace block stand within a courtyard enclosed by a curtain wall and gatehouse.

The basement of the old tower has two vaulted chambers, one a kitchen, the other a wine-cellar. The main entrance is at first-floor level, reached by an external stair. The thick walls, beside the original entrance, contain a small guardroom, with a trapdoor leading to a prison. The hall is a fine large chamber, with two stone benches running along the walls.

Dean Castle

The lands were given to the Boyds by Robert the Bruce in the 14th century. The castle is said to have been besieged by the English during the Wars of Independence. The old tower was built about 1460, although it probably incorporates earlier work. Robert Boyd became Guardian of James III during his minority, and practically ruled Scotland from 1466-9. He fell out of favour, however, and had to flee to Denmark, while Alexander, his brother, was executed for treason. William, 10th Lord Boyd, was created Earl of Kilmarnock in 1661.

William, 4th Earl, was Privy Councillor to Bonnie Prince Charlie during the Jacobite Rising of 1745. He was a Colonel in the Prince's guard, but was captured after the Battle of Culloden in 1746 and executed by beheading. Servants had been terrified by an apparition of Boyd's severed head rolling about the floor of Dean Castle before the Rising. When Boyd joined the Jacobites, he told James Stewart, 5th Earl of Galloway, about the haunting, who then correctly predicted Boyd would lose his head.

The lands were forfeited, but James, 5th Earl, recovered the estates in 1751, and seven years later became 15th Earl of Errol, taking the name Hay. Dean was sold and in 1735 a fire gutted the hall block.

The castle passed to Lord Howard de Walden in 1828. It was restored from 1905, and the entire building was donated by Lord Howard to the town of Kilmarnock in 1975. The castle now houses a museum with exhibits including a collection of armour and weapons and of musical instruments.

Dean Castle is surrounded 200 acres of public park with woodland walks, a herd of fallow deer, and an urban farm.

---

66 miles west and south of Edinburgh, 23 miles south-west of Glasgow, 1 mile north-east of Kilmarnock, off B7038, in Dean Castle County Park (signposted).

NS 437394   OS: 70   KA3 1XB

Open Apr-Sep, daily 11.00-17.00; open Oct to end Mar, Wed-Sun, 10.00-16.00; closed Christmas and New Year; park open, daily dawn-dusk.

Tel: 01563 554734   Web: www.deancastle.com

Features: Parking. Visitor centre (with gift shop, restaurant and WC; not at but near castle). Picnic area. Farm. Park. Woodland walks. Disabled access – but not into castle.

Nearest:

Dumfries House (17 miles)

Pollok House (20 miles)

Culzean Castle (28 miles)

Newark Castle (34 miles)

Brodick Castle, Arran (34 miles (ferry))

DELGATIE CASTLE

Colour photos page C19

DELGATIE

Inverness

Turriff

Aberdeen

An imposing, fascinating and largely unaltered old castle, Delgatie Castle incorporates a tower of five storeys dating from the 15th century, although possibly incorporating work from as early as 1030. The walls are very thick, the original windows are small, and there are many gunloops. There is an adjoining gabled house from the 16th century, and lower later buildings.

The castle has many original features. The entrance leads, through a fine vaulted vestibule, to a massive turnpike stair in one corner of the old tower, the widest in Britain. The basement is vaulted, and contains the old kitchen with a wide fireplace. The hall, on the first floor, is finely vaulted and is adorned with the Hay arms, and has a fireplace dated 1570. Excellent original painted ceilings survive on the second floor, dating from the late 16th century.

Delgatie was originally a property of the Comyn Earls of Buchan, but passed to the Hays in the 14th century, and they were made Earls of Errol in 1452. Sir Gilbert Hay of Delgatie, with many others of the family, was killed at the Battle of Flodden in 1513. Mary, Queen of Scots, spent three days here after the Battle of Corrichie in 1562, when the Gordons were defeated by her forces. Francis, 9th Earl, was summoned for treason in 1594 for supporting the Earl of Huntly, and part of the west wall was battered down by James VI's forces. The 9th Earl, however, went on to fight at Glenlivet in 1594, when the royal forces, under the Earl of Argyll, were defeated, but the rebellion ultimately

Delgatie Castle

Delgatie Castle, bedroom

failed and he was forfeited. Sir William Hay of Delgatie was standard bearer to the Marquis of Montrose, during his campaign of 1645. Although defeated at Philiphaugh, Hay managed to return the standard to Buchanan Castle, but he was executed with Montrose at Edinburgh in 1650, and buried beside him in St Giles Cathedral.

The Hays supported the Jacobites during the 1715 and 1745 Risings and suffered for it, Delgatie passing from the family in 1762, but the property was bought back and then made the Clan Hay centre in 1948.

The building is said to be haunted by a the ghost of a spirited young woman, known as Rohaise. She is thought to have defended the castle from an attack, and haunts the bedroom off the main stair, which now bears her name.

162 miles north of Edinburgh, 37 miles north and west of Aberdeen, 2 miles east of Turriff, off A947, at Delgatie Castle (signposted).
NJ 755506 OS: 29 AB53 5TD
Open all year, daily 10.00-17.00; closed for two weeks over Xmas and New Year. Venue for weddings and events. Self-catering apartments in castle and grounds. Trout fishery.
Tel: 01888 563479 Web: www.delgatiecastle.com
Features: Parking. Gift shop. Tearoom. WC. Disabled access to tearoom and front hall only. Admission charged.
Nearest:
Huntly Castle (22 miles)
Tolquhon Castle (23 miles)
Castle Fraser (32 miles)
Balvenie Castle (36 miles)
Kildrummy Castle (38 miles)

DIRLETON CASTLE

Colour photo page C20

Standing on a rock in picturesque grounds, Dirleton Castle consists of towers and ranges of buildings around a courtyard, which was once surrounded by a wide ditch. The old part of the castle, dating from the 13th century, is grouped around a small triangular court, and consists of a large drum tower, a smaller round tower and a rectangular tower. The chambers in the drum tower are polygonal, one on top of the other. The upper chamber, probably the lord's room, is a particularly fine apartment.

The entrance to the castle is by a wooden bridge across the wide ditch, and is through a gatehouse, formerly with a drawbridge and portcullis and protected by a murder hole. On one side of the castle is a range of buildings with a very thick outer wall, and the basement, partly dug out of solid rock. The kitchen has two huge fireplaces and the vast hall, reached by a modern wooden stair, is now very ruinous, although one unique feature is the stone-built buffet, probably reset in the current position. A stair leads down to the chapel and priest's room, below which is a dungeon, and beneath this is a claustrophobic pit-prison. A stair descends from the courtyard to the former gardens, now a bowling green surrounded by yew trees.

Dirleton Castle

Dirleton Castle, main entrance

There is a fine beehive doocot near the castle with more than 1,000 spaces for birds, and the original entrance gateway is now outside the perimeter wall.

The lands were held by the Congilton family before passing to the Vaux family about 1150. Dirleton was captured by the English after a hard siege in 1298. It was retaken by the Scots in 1311 and partly demolished, but was rebuilt and seized by the Earl of Douglas in 1363.

In the second half of the 14th century the castle passed by marriage to the Halyburton family, and James IV visited in 1505. In the 16th century it passed, again by marriage to, the Ruthvens, later Earls of Gowrie. After their forfeiture in 1600, following the Gowrie Conspiracy, the lands were acquired by Thomas Erskine of Gogar.

In 1649 several women and men, who had confessed to witchcraft after the witch-pricker, John Kincaid, had found devil's marks on them, were imprisoned in the castle, later to be strangled and burned at the stake.

The following year the castle was besieged by General Monck, during Cromwell's invasion of Scotland. A party of mosstroopers based at Dirleton had attacked Cromwell's lines of communication with some success, but they were quickly forced to surrender. Three of the leaders were subsequently shot.

In 1663 the property was bought by Sir John Nisbet, who built the house of Archerfield to replace Dirleton Castle. Archerfield is now a hotel. Dirleton Castle was given to The National Trust for Scotland in 1981 and is in the care of Historic Scotland.

There are fine gardens with ancient yews and hedges around the bowling green, as well as an exceptionally long flower border (believed to be the longest herbaceous border in the world) in the fine early 20th-century Arts and Crafts garden, as well as a recreated Victorian garden.

Dirleton Castle, Great Hall buffet

Dirleton is an attractive place with a village green, cafe, inn and hotel, and a church, dating from 17th century and with the classical Archerfield Aisle of 1650, in a picturesque spot. The church is open to the public.

23 miles east and north of Edinburgh, 2.5 miles west of North Berwick, off A198, Dirleton village (signposted).
NT 518840   OS: 66   EH39 5ER
Historic Scotland: open Apr-Sep, daily 9.30-17.30; Oct-Mar, daily 9.30-16.30; last ticket 30 mins before closing; closed 25/26 Dec and 1/2 Jan.
Tel: 01620 850330   Web: www.historic-scotland.gov.uk
Features: Parking nearby, 120 yard walk to castle. WC by parking. Shop. Refreshments. Limited wheelchair access to castle but gardens accessible. Fabulous gardens. Bowling green. Admission charged.
Tantallon Castle (5 miles)
Newhailes (18 miles)
Craigmillar Castle (21 miles)
Palace of Holyroodhouse (22 miles)
Crichton Castle (22 miles)

DOUNE CASTLE

Colour photo page C21

On a strong site in a lovely location above the River Teith, Doune Castle, built in the late 14th century, consists of two tall and strong towers linked by a lower range. These buildings form two sides of a courtyard, the other sides enclosed by a high curtain wall. Other ranges were planned to surround the whole courtyard, but were apparently never built. The curtain wall has open rounds at the corners, and corbelled-out semi-circular bartizans midway between the rounds.

The larger gatehouse, or lord's tower, with the arched entrance or pend to the castle through the basement, is rectangular in plan, with a semi-circular tower projecting at one corner. It rises to five storeys and 100 foot high, and a gabled garret within a flush parapet. The tower has vaulted cellars, and a fine vaulted hall on the first floor, reached by an external stone stair from the courtyard. The hall has a magnificent double fireplace and a minstrels' gallery, as well as a carved oak screen.

The smaller, or kitchen, tower rises to four storeys and a gabled garret, also within a flush parapet. This tower has an enormous arched fireplace, an oven and drains. Above this were private chambers, a suite of which was used by Mary, Queen of Scots.

Doune Castle

The joining range contains a lesser hall, and was also originally reached by a separate outside stair.

The castle was built by Robert Stewart, Duke of Albany, who virtually ruled Scotland during the reign of Robert III and the imprisonment in England of the young James I. When Albany died in 1420, his son, Murdoch, succeeded him as Regent and as Duke, but when James I was freed in 1424 he had Murdoch executed.

Doune was kept as a royal hunting lodge, prison, and dower house for the widows of James III, James IV and James V. It was occasionally used by Mary, Queen of Scots, and was held by forces loyal to her until 1570. This is another castle where a ghostly apparition of Mary has been reported. The property passed to the Earls of Moray.

Doune was occupied by the Marquis of Montrose in 1645, and by Government troops during the Jacobite Risings of 1689 and 1715. It was taken by Jacobites in 1745, and used as a prison, although many of the prisoners escaped. The castle was used as a location for *Monty Python and the Holy Grail*.

The ballad 'The Bonnie Earl o' Murray' tells the tale of the murder of James Stewart, the Earl of Moray, at Donibristle, by men sent by George Gordon, 6th Earl of Huntly, during a feud, and has the last verse:

'O lang will his Lady.
Look owre the Castle Doune.
Ere she see the Earl o' Moray
Come sounding through the toun.'

44 miles west and north of Edinburgh, 33 miles north and east of Glasgow, 8 miles north west of Stirling, 0.25 miles south-east of Doune, off A820, at Doune Castle (signposted).
NN 728011   OS: 57   FK16 6EA
Historic Scotland: open Apr-Sep, daily 9.30-17.30; Oct-Mar, Sat-Wed 9.30-16.30; last ticket 30 mins before closing; closed 25/26 Dec and 1/2 Jan.
Tel: 01786 841742   Web: www.historic-scotland.gov.uk
Features: Parking. Short walk to castle. Shop. Refreshments. WC. Disabled limited access. Nature trail. Admission charged.
Nearest:
Stirling Castle (8 miles)
Culross Palace (10 miles)
Drummond Castle Gardens (16 miles)
Castle Campbell (19 miles)
Callendar House (22 miles)

DRUM CASTLE

Colour photo page C21

One of the oldest occupied houses in Scotland and surrounded by extensive gardens, Drum Castle consists of a plain 13th-century tower of four storeys. To this has been added a large L-shaped range of 1619, and the castle was extended again in the 19th century.

The old tower has rounded thick walls, which are pierced by small windows, gunloops and slits. An external stone stair leads to the entrance at first-floor level. The vaulted basement is lit only by slits, and the main hall, which is also vaulted, is on the second floor.

Drum Castle

Drum Castle

The 17th-century extension consists of an L-shaped range of three storeys and a garret, with square gabled projecting towers and a round stair-tower. There are other additions, which together with the older parts, form a courtyard completed by a curtain wall with a gateway.

The basement of the extension is vaulted, and contained the kitchen with a large fireplace and cellars.

There is a walled garden with old roses, and in the grounds is the Old Wood of Drum, an ancient oak woodland.

Drum was a property of the Crown and the tower may have been built by Alexander III. It was held by the Irvines from 1323, when the lands were given to them by Robert the Bruce after Sir William de Irwyn, or Irvine, whose seat was at Bonshaw, had been his standard bearer. The Irvines were much involved in the feuding between the Keiths and the Forbeses. The Irvines apparently burned down Hallforest Castle in revenge for the death of one of their family, and this came to battle at Keiths Muir, at which battle many of the Keiths were slain.

Sir Alexander Irvine, 3rd Laird, was killed at the Battle of Harlaw in 1411, slain by and slaying MacLean of Duart, Red Hector of the Battles. His brother (who then changed his name to Alexander) married into the Keiths, so ending that feud. The eldest son of the 6th Laird, another Alexander, was slain at the Battle of Pinkie in 1547. Alexander, 10th Laird, supported Charles I, and Drum was besieged and plundered by Archibald Campbell, 8th Earl and 1st Marquis of Argyll, in 1644, and ransacked again the following year when the womenfolk were turned out of the castle.

Alexander, 11th Laird, caused a scandal when he married Margaret Coutts, a sixteen-year-old local shepherdess (and forty-seven years younger than him), after the death of his wife. They went on to have three daughters, and the events are featured in the old ballad 'The Laird o' Drum'.

The family were Jacobites, and fought in the 1715 and 1745 Jacobite Risings. Alexander, 14th Laird, died from wound received at the Battle of Sheriffmuir in 1715; and Alexander, 17th of Drum, fought at Culloden, although he managed to escape both the aftermath of the battle and forfeiture, after hiding in a secret chamber at Drum and spending several years in exile in France.

128 miles north of Edinburgh, 13 miles west and south of Aberdeen, 3 miles west of Peterculter, off A93, at Drum Castle (signposted).
NJ 796005   OS: 38   AB31 5EY
NTS: open Apr-Jun & Sep-Oct, Thu-Mon 11.00-16.00; Jul & Aug, daily 11.00-16.00, last entry 45 mins before closing; grounds all year, daily 9.30-sunset. Entry to Drum Castle may be restricted because of essential conservation work (2013).
Tel: 0844 493 2161   Web: www.nts.org.uk
Features: Parking. Gift shop. Tearoom. WC. Disabled facilities. Garden of historic roses. Woodland walks. Admission charged.
Nearest:
Crathes Castle (6 miles)
Castle Fraser (13 miles)
Dunnottar Castle (17 miles)
Craigievar Castle (22 miles)
Edzell Castle (31 miles)

DRUMLANRIG CASTLE

Colour photos pages C22 & C23

Glasgow Edinburgh

DRUMLANRIG
Thornhill

Dumfries

In a prominent position in lovely parkland and wooded grounds, Drumlanrig Castle is a Scottish baronial mansion house, which dates from the 17th century. The castle has four ranges around a courtyard, with higher rectangular towers at the corners, crowned by pepper-pot turrets.

In the middle of the 14th century the Barony of Drumlanrig was held by the Earls of Mar, but when James Douglas, 2nd Earl of Douglas and Mar, died at Otterburn in 1388, the property passed to William, his son, who became the first Laird of Drumlanrig.

The original castle was built by the Douglases soon after 1357, but was sacked by the English in 1549. It was then slighted in 1575 because the family had supported Mary, Queen of Scots, who had stayed here in 1563. Drumlanrig was restored and rebuilt, as James VI visited in 1617.

The new castle was built between 1679 and 1691 by William Douglas, 3rd Earl of Queensberry, who was made Duke in 1684. The Duke, however, spent

Drumlanrig Castle

Drumlanrig Castle, main entrance

only one night in his splendid new mansion, decided he did not like it, and moved back to Sanquhar Castle, where he died in 1695. His son, James, 2nd Duke, transferred his seat to Drumlanrig. Bonnie Prince Charlie stayed here in 1745 after retreat from Derby, and his men damaged the building and slashed a painting of William of Orange.

Drumlanrig passed to the Scott Dukes of Buccleuch in 1810 after the death of William, 4th Duke of Queensberry, known as Old Q, whose portrait by Allan Ramsay hangs in the Drawing Room. The castle was restored in 1827, and service wings were added by the architect William Burn. There is a fine collection of pictures, including paintings by Rembrandt and Holbein, as well as many other works of art.

Drumlanrig is still owned by the Montagu-Douglas-Scott Dukes of Buccleuch and Queensberry, who hold many titles, including Marquess of Dumfriesshire, Earl of Drumlanrig, Buccleuch, Sanquhar and Dalkeith, and Viscount Nith, Torthorwald and Ross.

Three ghosts are said to haunt the castle. One is reputed to be the spirit of Lady Anne Douglas, seen with her head under her arm, another that of a young woman in a flowing dress, and the third that of a monkey.

Drumlanrig Castle, Dining Room

63 miles south-west of Edinburgh, 61 miles south of Glasgow, 18 miles north of Dumfries, 3 miles north and west of Thornhill, off A76, at Drumlanrig Castle (signposted).
NX 851992   OS: 78   DG3 4AQ
Castle open for guided tours May-Aug, daily 11.00 to last tour at 16.00; castle open at other times for groups by arrangement; country park open 10.00-17.00 (also open in winter: check with castle). Weddings and private events. Field sports. Landrover tours. Fishing.
Tel: 01848 331555   Web: www.drumlanrigcastle.co.uk
Features: Parking. Shop. Tea room. WC. Disabled access to castle. Park land, woodland walks and gardens. Adventure playground. Admission charged.
Nearest:
Caerlaverock Castle (27 miles)
Dumfries House (29 miles)
Dean Castle (43 miles)
Cardoness Castle (44 miles)
Culzean Castle (50 miles)

DRUMMOND CASTLE

Colour photos page C24

Crieff • • Perth
DRUMMOND
Glasgow Edinburgh

Built on a rocky outcrop, Drummond Castle consists of an ancient tower of five storeys and gatehouse, dating from the 15th century with later work, and a late 18th-century mansion. The old tower has a corbelled-out parapet. The magnificent gardens are laid out in the form of a Renaissance garden of the 17th century with parterres, formal terraces, statues, urns and fountains. The gardens were abandoned after the Jacobite Risings but were restored early in the 19th century, and then again in the 20th century.

Sir Malcolm Drummond distinguished himself at the Battle of Bannockburn in 1314, and was given the lands here, originally known as Concraig. Margaret Drummond – daughter of the then laird – was a lover of James IV, and they were reputedly married and had a daughter. Some of the nobles wanted James to marry Margaret Tudor, sister of Henry VIII, and form an alliance with England. To this end, and to 'free' James, Margaret and two of her sisters were murdered with poisoned sugared fruit, and are buried side by side in Dunblane Cathedral, where there is a memorial to them in the floor of the church. In 1490 William Drummond, her brother and second son of Lord Drummond, was executed after he torched Monzievaird Church, killing more than 150 Murrays, including women and children.

Mary, Queen of Scots, visited the castle in 1566-7 with the Earl of Bothwell, and the Drummonds were made Earls of Perth in 1605. The castle was badly damaged by Cromwell in the 1650s, then restored, to be slighted after having been occupied by Hanoverian troops during the Jacobite Rising of 1715. James, 4th Earl, was made Duke of Perth by James VII in the Jacobite peerage. James,

Drummond Castle Gardens

79

Drummond Castle

5th Earl, had commanded the Jacobite cavalry at the Battle of Sheriffmuir that year, and the 6th, another James, commanded the left wing of the Jacobite army at the Battle of Culloden in 1746. The family was forfeited as a result.

The castle passed by marriage to the Barons Willoughby de Eresby, created Earls of Ancaster in 1892 (the family name is Heathcote-Drummond-Willoughby). The castle was restored in 1822, when a turreted extension was added to the mansion, and Queen Victoria and Prince Albert visited in 1842. The castle and magnificent formal garden featured in the 1995 film version of *Rob Roy* with Liam Neeson.

51 miles north-west of Edinburgh, 22 miles west of Perth, 2.5 miles south and west of Crieff, 3 miles north-west of Muthill, off A822, at Drummond Castle (signposted).
NN 844181 OS: 58 PH7 4HZ
Gardens open Easter wknd and/or May-Oct 13.00-18.00; last admission 17.00. Drummond Castle is not open to the public.
Tel: 01764 681433 Web: www.drummondcastlegardens.co.uk
Features: Parking. Shop. Refreshments. WC. Disabled partial access. Picnic benches. Admission charged.
Doune Castle (16 miles)
Huntingtower (19 miles)
Castle Campbell (23 miles)
Scone Palace (24 miles)
Elcho Castle (25 miles)

DUART CASTLE

Colour photos page C25

An extremely impressive and daunting fortress, Duart Castle consists of a large 13th-century curtain wall, enclosing a courtyard on a rocky knoll. In 1360 Lachlan Lubanach, 5th Chief, built the squat tower on the outside of the curtain wall. There are later ranges of buildings, and the entrance was through a gatehouse and portcullis.

The tower has very thick walls. The main hall, on the first floor, has a great fireplace and round-headed windows with stone seats. The upper floors are reached by a narrow turnpike stair in the thickness of the wall.

The Macleans of Duart claim descent from Gillean of the Battle Axe. Lachlan Lubanach married Elizabeth, daughter of the Lord of the Isles, granddaughter of Robert II King of Scots, and was granted the first known charter for Duart dated 1360 as her dowry. While fighting with the MacDonalds, the 6th Chief Red Hector was killed at the Battle of Harlaw in 1411, slaying and being slain by Sir Alexander Irvine of Drum. The 9th Chief was slain at Flodden in 1513.

Lachlan Cattanach, 11th Chief, was so unhappy with Catherine Campbell, his wife, that he had the poor woman chained to a rock in the Firth of Lorn to be drowned at high tide. However, she was rescued and taken to her father, Archibald Campbell, 2nd Earl of Argyll. As a result, Maclean was murdered in his bed in Edinburgh by her brother, Sir John Campbell of Cawdor, in 1523.

In 1604 Sir Hector Og Maclean of Duart, along with other chiefs, was kidnapped and imprisoned while being entertained aboard ship off Aros Castle. Sir Lachlan Maclean was made a baronet of Nova Scotia in 1631, and his son, Sir Hector, was killed at the Battle of Inverkeithing in 1651. In 1674 the castle

Duart Castle

81

Duart Castle

was acquired by the Campbell Earl of Argyll, who also got most of their lands, although not without much bloodshed in the next few years. The Macleans remained staunch supporters of the Stewarts throughout the Jacobite Risings, and fought at Killiecrankie in 1689 and in the later rebellions; by then the remaining lands on Mull had gone to the Campbells. Although garrisoned, the castle was not used as a residence, and was abandoned after the Jacobite Rising of 1745 to become derelict and roofless.

Duart was acquired in 1911 by Sir Fitzroy Maclean, who restored the castle, and it is still owned by the Macleans of Duart and Morvern.

Duart was used as a location in the Powell and Pressburger romance *I Know Where I am Going* with Wendy Hiller and Roger Livesey, the Anthony Hopkins film *When Eight Bells Toll*, and the Sean Connery and Catherine Zeta-Jones movie *Entrapment*.

113 miles north-west of Glasgow, 136 miles west and north of Edinburgh, east side of island of Mull (regular CalMac ferry from Oban), 3 miles south of Craignure, off A849, at Duart Castle (signposted). NM 749354   OS: 49   PA64 6AP

Open Apr-mid Oct: Apr, Sun-Thu 11.00-16.00 + Easter weekend Fri-Mon; open May-mid Oct, daily 10.30-17.00

Tel: 01680 812309   Web: www.duartcastle.com

Features: Ferry from Oban on mainland to Craignure on Mull, castle coach runs to Duart three times daily to coincide with ferries. Parking. Tea room and gift shop. WC. Picnic areas. Disabled access to tea room and gift shop. Admission charged for entry to castle (tea room and gift shop free entry). Combined tickets through CalMac in Oban (ferry, coach and entry) or from coach (coach and entry).

Nearest:

Dunstaffnage Castle (19 miles (ferry))

Kilchurn Castle (37 miles (ferry))

Carnasserie Castle (43 miles (ferry))

Inveraray Castle (53 miles (ferry))

Skipness Castle (76 miles (ferry))

DUFF HOUSE

Colour photo page C29

Banff
DUFF HOUSE
Inverness
Aberdeen

D uff House is a fine classical mansion with colonnades and corner towers, dating from 1735, and designed by the architect William Adam for William Duff of Braco, later Earl of Fife. Adam and Duff fell out over the cost of building the house, and work stopped in 1741 – the subsequent legal action was eventually won by Adam, although at great cost to both. William Duff never lived at Duff House, preferring Rothiemay Castle, near Huntly, (which, although a great house, was demolished in 1956), where he died in 1763. He was a Member of Parliament for Banffshire from 1727-34, and supported the Crown during the Jacobite Risings, although his heir supported Bonnie Prince Charlie.

James, 2nd Earl, was also a Member of Parliament for Banffshire, and he made Duff House his home and completed the building. James was the second son of Duff, the first son William, the Jacobite, had died unmarried in 1753.

Alexander Duff, 6th Earl, was made 1st Duke of Fife and Marquess of Macduff in 1889 when he married Princess Louise, the oldest daughter of the

Duff House

future Edward VII and granddaughter of Queen Victoria. Duff was very wealthy, but in 1911 died of pneumonia after he and his family were shipwrecked on their way to Egypt.

The Duffs did not live at the house after 1906, and it was then rented out for uses including a hotel and a hospital for the treatment of internal diseases. The house was requisitioned by the army during World War II, including use as a POW camp and then as a headquarters for various British regiments.

The house was damaged by German bombing in 1940. Two incendiary bombs penetrated the roof but did not go off, but a later service wing at the rear of the house was seriously damaged and was subsequently demolished.

By the 1950s the house was derelict but it was restored in the 1990s and is now used to display works of art from the National Galleries of Scotland. The house is part of a designed landscape, and there are walks in the grounds, as well as the gothic mausoleum, Bridge of Alvah, the Temple of Venus on the hill at Macduff overlooking the house, and the ice house. The gates of the house were moved to Banff Castle on the High Street of Dufftown.

The building is said to have a Green Lady.

165 miles north of Edinburgh, 45 miles north and west of Aberdeen, south of Banff, off A97, at Duff House (signposted).
NJ 692633   OS: 29   AB45 3SX
Open Apr-Sep, daily 11.00-17.00; Nov-Mar, Thu-Sun; venue for weddings and functions.
Tel: 01261 818181   Web: www.duffhouse.org.uk
Features: Parking. Shop. Tea room. WC. Picnic area. Disabled facilities including lift and toilets. Admission charged (free admission to shop, tearoom, grounds and woodland walks).
Nearest:
Delgatie Castle (11 miles)
Huntly Castle (21 miles)
Tolquhon Castle (31 miles)
Balvenie Castle (31 miles)
Kildrummy Castle (37 miles)

DUMFRIES HOUSE

Colour photos page C26

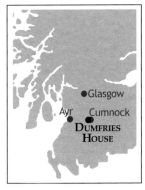

Dumfries House is an elegant and beautifully proportioned classical mansion, rising to three storeys in the main block and with two lower flanking pavilions. This was the first complete mansion designed by the architect Robert Adam. It was built in 1754 for William Crichton-Dalrymple, 5th Earl of Dumfries, and work was supervised by John Adam, Robert's brother – it was their first independent commission.

The house has a sumptuous interior with ornate plasterwork, marble fireplaces and lavish furnishings, including pieces by Thomas Chippendale.

The property was originally known as Lochnorris or Leifnorris, and there was an old tower, a property of the Crawfords in 1440. The tower was demolished in 1771, although it stood to the north of the house, near the stables, and furniture from the old house is on display in Dumfries House. In 1635 William Crichton, 1st Earl of Dumfries, purchased the estate, and the property passed through marriage to the Dalrymples.

By marriage to the heiress Elizabeth Penelope Crichton, Dumfries House then went to John Stuart, Viscount Mountstuart, although both he and his

Dumfries House

Dumfries House, Eagle Table

wife died young. They had a son, John, later 2nd Marquess of Bute, who went on to inherit both Mountstuart and Dumfries House. The 3rd Marquess, his son and also called John, was one of the richest men of his day. He extended Dumfries House, roughly doubling the size, but done so that the additions are not apparent from the front of the house. He spent, however, more attention on his other properties, including Mount Stuart on Bute and Cardiff Castle.

Dumfries House remained with his descendants until Johnny Dumfries, the 7th Earl and a racing driver, decided to sell Dumfries House and concentrate on Mount Stuart. In 2007 Dumfries House was bought and is now managed by the Great Steward of Scotland's Dumfries House Trust.

The house is said to be haunted by a smelly ghost, which makes its presence felt by exuding an unholy stench. Another tale is that of a phantom coach, linked to the Hastings family who were related by marriage to the Marquesses of Bute. Whenever one of the Hastings family was near death, the story is that a phantom coach would be heard or seen, approaching the doors of the place where they were staying. One report at Dumfries House comes from the death of the 3rd Marquess of Bute in 1900, when his daughter is reputed to have heard the coach outside the house.

Dumfries House

38 miles south of Glasgow, 63 miles west and south of Edinburgh, 2 miles west of Cumnock, off A70, Dumfries House (signposted).
NS 541204 OS: 70 KA18 2NJ
Open for guided tours Apr-Oct, daily (although check Sat), last admission 15.30; Nov-Mar, open Sat & Sun only, tours at 12.15 and 13.45. Venue for weddings and events. Guest house and self-catering cottages.
Tel: 01290 425959 Web: dumfries-house.org.uk
Features: Parking. Gift shop. Tea room. WC. Disabled access to the ground and first floor. Walks. Admission charged.
Nearest:
Dean Castle (17 miles)
Culzean Castle (25 miles)
Drumlanrig Castle (28 miles)
Craignethan Castle (33 miles)
Pollok House (35 miles)

DUNNOTTAR CASTLE

Colour photos page C27

Aberdeen
Stonehaven •
DUNNOTTAR •
Dundee •

On a virtually impregnable cliff-top promontory some 160 feet above the sea, Dunnottar Castle is a spectacular ruined courtyard castle, parts of which date from the 12th century, although there was probably a stronghold here from the earliest times. The entrance is through a doorway, defended by a portcullis, and several rows of gunloops, and then up a flight of steps and through a tunnel.

The large site has many buildings, including an L-plan tower from the 15th century and ranges built around a large courtyard, enclosing a bowling green, a large chapel, a stable block, a forge, barracks, and a priest's house.

A castle here was captured by William Wallace from the English in 1296, one story relating that he burnt 4000 Englishmen. Edward III of England took Dunnottar in the 1330s and strengthened it, but it was quickly recaptured by Sir Andrew Moray, the Regent. The Keiths acquired the property in 1382. William Keith, 5th Earl Marischal, was a noted scholar, and founded Marischal College in Aberdeen. Mary, Queen of Scots, stayed here in 1562.

William, 9th Earl, entertained King Charles II at Dunnottar in 1650, and the following year the Scottish crown jewels were brought to the castle for

Dunnottar Castle

Dunnottar Castle, entrance

safety during Cromwell's invasion of Scotland. General Lambert besieged the castle in 1652, but this proved extremely difficult, and the castle was only reduced after eight months by starvation and mutiny. The regalia and state papers were smuggled out to be hidden in nearby Kinneff Church until recovered at the Restoration in 1660.

In 1685 Covenanters, numbering some 167 women and men, were packed into one of the cellars during a hot summer and nine died while 25 escaped. The others, when freed, were found to have been tortured. There is a memorial in Dunnottar Parish Church to those who died.

The Earl Marischal threw in his lot with the Stewarts during the Jacobite rising of 1715, and was subsequently forfeited. The Duke of Argyll partly destroyed Dunnottar in 1716, and it was more fully slighted in 1718. Between the wars, the castle was consolidated and partly reroofed. External shots of the castle were used for the film *Hamlet* with Mel Gibson.

Sightings of several ghosts have been reported, including the apparition of a girl, around 13 years old and dressed in a dull plaid-type dress. Other ghosts are said to include a young deer hound and a tall Scandinavian-looking man.

110 miles north and east of Edinburgh, 19 miles south of Aberdeen, 2 miles south of Stonehaven, off A92, at Dunnottar Castle (signposted).
NO 882839   OS: 45   AB3 2TL
Open Apr-Sep, daily 9.00-18.00; Oct-Mar, daily 10.00-15.00; last admission 30 mins before closing; opening is weather dependant (tel to check in winter) and closed 25 & 26 Dec and 1 & 2 Jan.
Tel: 01569 762173   Web: www.dunnottarcastle.co.uk
Features: Parking. Getting to the castle involves a walk, steep climb, and a steeper one back. Shop. Castle Picnic Van (Jun-mid Sep) at car park. WC. Admission charged.
Nearest:
Crathes Castle (16 miles)
Drum Castle (17 miles)
Castle Fraser (25 miles)
Craigievar Castle (35 miles)
Haddo House (38 miles)

Dunnottar Castle

DUNROBIN CASTLE

Colour photos page C28

Dunrobin Castle is an elegant fairy-tale castle and stately home in a lovely location among splendid formal gardens with a fountain.

The castle incorporates an altered 15th-century tower – parts of which may date from the 1300s – and 17th-century courtyard mansion, with round corner turrets, which was greatly enlarged in the 18th and 19th centuries. The tower is vaulted on all floors, and

Dunrobin Castle

Dunrobin Castle, gardens

still has its original iron yett. With the tower, the 17th-century L-plan block of three storeys and a garret formed a courtyard. A large round tower joins up this block and the tower. The castle was remodelled and enlarged between 1845 and 1851, and again in 1915-21 by Sir Robert Lorimer.

The Sutherland family were made Earls of Sutherland in 1235, and Kenneth, 4th Earl and Regent of Scotland, fell at the Battle of Halidon Hill in England in 1333. William, the next Earl, was murdered in a feud with the Mackays, and the 6th Earl, Robert or Robin, is believed to have built the first castle, which is named after him. John, 8th Earl, was declared unfit, and the earldom passed to the Gordons. Isobel Sinclair poisoned John, 11th Earl, and his wife at Helmsdale Castle, hoping to secure the succession of her son, but the future 12th Earl escaped and, instead, she managed to poison her own son; she committed suicide before she could be executed. The young Earl of Sutherland was captured by the Earl of Caithness and forced to marry Lady Barbara Sinclair, who was twice his age. When he came of age, he divorced her, and assumed the title. John, 16th Earl, supported the Hanoverians in the Jacobite Rising. The Jacobites seized Dunrobin, but they soon surrendered.

The male line of the Sutherlands failed, and the property went through an heiress to the Marquess of Stafford, and they were made Dukes of Sutherland in 1833. Done for whatever motives, the family are remembered for their part in the Clearances, when many of their own tenants were thrown off their lands. The 3rd Duke contributed much of his money to the building of the railway to the north. The male line failed again, and the earldom and dukedom have parted company: the earldom and castle passed to the present Countess of Sutherland, while the dukedom went to the next male heir, the Earl of Ellesmere. During World War I the castle was used as a naval hospital, and then as a boy's public school between 1965 and 1972.

The upper floors of the castle are reputedly haunted by the spectre of Margaret, a daughter of John, 14th Earl, who died in 1679 (he also had a daughter called Jean, but she is recorded as being married in 1657). Margaret decided to elope with her lover but her father, who considered the man unsuitable for his daughter, found out, and had her imprisoned in one of the attic rooms. She tried to escape by climbing down a rope, but her father surprised her and she fell to her death.

206 miles north of Edinburgh, 50 miles north of Inverness, 1 mile north-east of Golspie, south of A9, at Dunrobin Castle (signposted). NC 852008   OS: 17   KW10 6SF

Open Apr-May and Sep-mid Oct, Mon-Sat 10.30-16.30, Sun 12.00-16.30; Jun-Aug, daily 10.30-17.00; last entry 30 mins before closing; venue for weddings and events.

Tel: 01408 633177   Web: www.dunrobincastle.co.uk

Features: Parking. Gift shop. Restaurant. WC. Disabled access: phone to arrange. Museum with a collection of Pictish stones. Formal gardens. Falconry displays. Admission charged.

Nearest:

Cawdor Castle (64 miles)

Castle of Mey (70 miles)

Brodie Castle (74 miles)

Balvenie Castle (106 miles)

Eilean Donan Castle (107 miles)

DUNSTAFFNAGE CASTLE

Colour photo page C29

O n a promontory in the Firth of Lorn said to have once been an island, Dunstaffnage Castle consists of a massive 13th-century curtain wall, with round towers, and an altered 16th-century gatehouse. The wall is 60 foot high in places, crowned by a parapet, and is pierced by arrow slits. Ranges of buildings within the walls contained a hall and kitchen. In 1725 a two-storey house was added, which was altered in the 19th century.

A stronghold here was held by the kings of Dalriada in the 7th century, and was possibly one of the places where the Stone of Destiny was kept. The present castle was built by the MacDougalls, and it was besieged and captured by Robert the Bruce in 1309 after the MacDougalls had been defeated at the Pass of Brander. Bruce made the castle royal property with the Campbells as keepers.

Dunstaffnage Castle

Dunstaffnage Castle

James IV visited twice, and Alexander Campbell, captain of the castle, was slain at Flodden in 1513. Archibald Campbell, 9th Earl of Argyll, burned the castle in 1685 during his rebellion of the same year. In 1715 and 1746 government troops occupied the castle during the Jacobite Risings, and Flora MacDonald was briefly imprisoned here after helping Bonnie Prince Charlie.

There is a fine ruined chapel nearby in an atmospheric setting, dating from the 13th century, which incorporates the Campbell burial aisle, dated 1740.

The castle is said to be haunted by a ghost in a green dress, and her appearance reputedly heralds events, both bad and good, in the lives of the Campbells. Her heavy footfalls have been reported.

96 miles north-west of Glasgow, 120 miles west and north of Edinburgh, 3.5 miles north-east of Oban, off A85 at Dunbeg, at Dunstaffnage Castle (signposted).
NM 882344 OS: 49 PA37 1PZ
Historic Scotland: open Apr-Sep, daily 9.30-17.30; Oct-Mar, Sat-Wed 9.30-16.30, closed Thu & Fri; last ticket 30 mins before closing; closed 25/26 Dec and 1/2 Jan.
Tel: 01631 562465 Web: www.historic-scotland.gov.uk
Features: Parking. Gift shop. Refreshments. WC. Disabled access around grounds and shop but not into castle. Admission charged.
Duart, Castle Mull (19 miles (ferry))
Kilchurn Castle (21 miles)
Carnasserie Castle (31 miles)
Inveraray Castle (36 miles)
Skipness Castle (66 miles)

DUNVEGAN CASTLE

Colour photo page C30

On what was once an island in Loch Dunvegan, Dunvegan Castle is the much photographed stronghold of the chiefs of MacLeod. The castle has a massive 14th-century tower and the 16th-century Fairy Tower, built by Alasdair Crotach, whose fine tomb is at St Clement's Church at Rodel Church on Harris. To this was added a joining hall block in the 17th century, and there is also a later wing. The castle was completely restored in 1840-50, and then given ornamental turrets and modern battlements.

The castle has been continuously occupied by the chiefs of MacLeod since 1270, who trace their ancestry back to Leod, a son of Olaf the Black, Viking king of the Isle of Man. The MacLeods supported Robert the Bruce in the Wars of Independence, and they fought at the bloody Battle of Harlaw in 1411. Dunvegan was visited by James V in 1540, and the king was reputedly entertained on the top of MacLeod's Tables, flat-topped hills, which dominate

Dunvegan Castle

that part of Skye. The MacLeods fought in 1651 at the Battle of Worcester for Charles II but lost 500 men, which made them reluctant to take part in the Jacobite Risings. In fact MacLeod of Dunvegan refused to join Bonnie Prince Charlie unless he had significant French help, which was perhaps wise, and the MacLeods did not take part in the Rising.

The castle is still owned by the chiefs of MacLeod.

Dunvegan is the home to the famous Fairy Flag, *Am Bratach Sith* in Gaelic. There are many legends surrounding this piece of silk, which is now reduced in size (from pieces being removed and kept for luck). One story is that it was given to one of the chiefs by his fairy wife at their parting. This is said to have taken place at the Fairy Bridge, three miles to the north east, at a meeting of rivers and roads. The chief had married his wife thinking she was a mortal woman, but she was only permitted to stay with him for 20 years before returning to Fairyland.

The flag, however, originates from the Middle East, and it has been dated to between 400 and 700 AD, predating the castle by hundreds of years. The flag is believed to give victory to the clan whenever unfurled, and reputedly did so at the battles of Glendale in 1490 and at Trumpan in 1580. The Fairy Flag was also believed to make the marriage of the MacLeods fruitful, when draped on the wedding bed, and to charm the herrings out of Dunvegan Loch when unfurled. Belief in its power was such that during World War II pilots from the clan carried a picture of the flag as a talisman.

Other interesting items at Dunvegan include a drinking horn, Rory Mor's Horn, holding several pints of claret, which the heir of the MacLeods had to empty in one go; and the Dunvegan Cup, gifted to the clan by the O'Neils of Ulster in 1596. There are also mementoes of Bonnie Prince Charlie and Flora MacDonald, and information about St Kilda, which was formerly a property of the family.

---

249 miles north-west of Edinburgh, 128 miles west of Inverness, 124 miles west and north of Fort William, 24 miles north-west of Portree, on island of Skye (accessible by bridge (A87) or by CalMac ferry from Mallaig), off A850, at Dunvegan Castle (signposted).
NG 247491 OS: 23 IV55 8WF
Open Apr-mid Oct, daily 10.00-17.30; last entry 30 mins before closing; mid Oct-Mar open for groups by appt only, Mon-Fri only; closed Xmas and New Year. Venue for weddings and events.
Tel: 01470 521206 Web: www.dunvegancastle.com
Features: Parking. Gift shops. Restaurant. WC. Gardens. Disabled access to castle entrance and gardens and ground floor and gun court accessible with help. Admission charged. Boat trips to seal colony. Holiday cottages available.
Nearest:
Eilean Donan Castle (59 miles)
Cawdor Castle (139 miles)
Brodie Castle (149 miles)
Dunrobin Castle (158 miles)
Ballindalloch Castle (173 miles)

EDINBURGH CASTLE

Colour photos page C30 & C31

Perched on a high rock, Edinburgh Castle was one of the strongest and most important castles in Scotland and, although the present complex of buildings dates from no earlier than the 15th century, it has a long and bloody history. This is also Scotland's most popular paid-for tourist attraction with more than 1,000,000 visits every year.

There was a fortress on the castle rock from the earliest times, but the oldest building is a small Norman chapel of the early 12th century, dedicated to St Margaret, wife of Malcolm Canmore. After Malcolm's death at Alnwick in 1093, and then Margaret's a few days later, the castle was besieged by his brother, Donald Bane, in support of his claim to the throne. Margaret's body was smuggled out and buried in Dunfermline Abbey. In 1173, after the capture of William I the Lion at Alnwick, the castle was surrendered to the English, but later recovered by the Scots.

The castle had an English garrison from 1296 until 1313 during the Wars of Independence, when the Scots, led by Thomas Randolph, climbed the rock, surprised the garrison, and retook it. The castle was slighted, but there was an English garrison here again until 1341, when it was retaken by a Scottish force disguised as merchants bringing provisions to the garrison. In 1367-71 David II rebuilt the castle with strong curtain walls and towers, and a large L-plan keep, David's Tower, which was named after him.

Edinburgh Castle (1900)

Edinburgh Castle

After the murder of William, the young 6th Earl of Douglas, and his brother David at the Black Dinner at the castle in 1440, it was attacked and captured by the Douglases after a nine-month siege, and required substantial repairs. James III's brother, Alexander, Duke of Albany, escaped after being imprisoned in David's Tower in 1479. James, himself, was confined in the tower by his nobles in 1482, but Alexander returned from exile, took his side, and had him released.

A new great hall was built in 1483, and other repairs were executed, but increasingly the royal palaces were favoured as comfortable residences over the castle – although the castle remained of vital importance as the state armoury, prison, record repository, and major fortress of Edinburgh.

In 1566 Mary, Queen of Scots, gave birth to the future James VI in the castle. After her abdication, it was held on her behalf, until English help forced it to surrender in 1573. Having been badly damaged by artillery, the castle was rebuilt to such an extent afterwards, and in subsequent periods, that all that survives of David's Tower is embedded in the Half Moon Battery.

The castle was captured in 1640 after a three-month siege by Covenanters, and Cromwell besieged it throughout the autumn of 1650. Much new work on the fortifications was done by Charles II, and many of the present buildings date from the 17th and 18th centuries. The Jacobites failed to take it in both the 1715 and 1745 Jacobite Risings, although some of them were incarcerated in it later, as were Napoleonic prisoners of war in the early 19th century.

The castle is the home of the Scottish crown jewels, and the Stone of Destiny – on which the Kings of Scots were inaugurated, and among many other attractions is the huge cannon Mons Meg, the Scottish War Memorial and the Regimental Museum of the Royal Scots. The castle remains a fascinating complex of buildings with spectacular views over the capital. The esplanade,

Edinburgh Castle

below the castle, is used during August for the Edinburgh military tattoo. The one o'clock gun is fired (virtually) every day from the castle walls.

The castle is reputedly haunted by many ghosts, including a headless drummer, a ghostly piper sent to search a tunnel leading down towards the High Street, phantoms of prisoners in the vaults, and the spectre of a dog whose remains are buried in the pets cemetery. One account also has the place haunted by a spectre of Mary, Queen of Scots, while the esplanade has the ghost of Janet Douglas, Lady Glamis, who was burnt to death here in 1537 after being accused of witchcraft and treason.

In the centre of Edinburgh, 46 miles east of Glasgow, off A1 (Princes Street), just west of Waverley Station, at top of Royal Mile (Castlehill), at Edinburgh Castle (signposted).
NT 252735 OS: 66 EH1 2NG
Historic Scotland: open Apr-Sep, daily 9.30-18.00; Oct-Mar, daily 9.30-17.00; times may be altered during Tattoo and state occasions; closed 25/26 Dec; open 1 Jan 11.00-17.00; last entry 60 mins before closing. The castle can be hired.
Tel: 0131 225 9846 Web: www.edinburghcastle.gov.uk
Features: Limited parking (no parking during tattoo). Shops. Restaurant and cafe. WC. Partial disabled access and mobility vehicle available. Admission charged.
Nearest:
Palace of Holyroodhouse (1 mile)
Craigmillar Castle (4 miles)
Lauriston Castle (5 miles)
Newhailes (6 miles)
Crichton Castle (15 miles)

EDZELL CASTLE

Colour photo page C32

A large and impressive building, Edzell Castle has an early 16th-century tower house, later enlarged and extended with ranges of buildings around a courtyard. A large pleasance, or garden, was created in 1604, and was surrounded by an ornamental wall, to which a summerhouse and a bath-house were added. The carved decoration of the garden walls is unique.

The L-plan tower, at one corner of the main courtyard, rises to four storeys and a garret, and has corbelled-out open rounds at all corners and small projecting half-rounds at the centre of each wall.

The entrance, reached through an arched doorway from the courtyard, is in the re-entrant angle. It leads to the vaulted basement, one cellar having a small stair to the hall on the first floor above. The hall has two fireplaces and the upper floors were reached by a wide stair.

The lands passed by marriage from the Stirlings of Glenesk to the Lindsay Earls of Crawford in 1357. Mary, Queen of Scots, held a Privy Council at Edzell in 1562, and stayed in the castle. Cromwell garrisoned it in 1651. During

Edzell Castle

Edzell Castle, garden

the Royalist uprising of 1653, John Lindsay was kidnapped from Edzell, but he was rescued by Cromwell's forces.

The Lindsays had to sell the property in 1715, because of huge debts, and it was bought by the Maule Earl of Panmure. The Maules were forfeited for their part in the 1745 Jacobite Rising, and the castle was garrisoned by Hanoverian troops, who did much damage. The Maules recovered Edzell in 1764, but the castle was abandoned soon afterwards.

The castle is said to be haunted by a White Lady, reputedly the spirit of Catherine Campbell, second wife of David Lindsay, 9th Earl of Crawford. She apparently died in 1578, but is said to have been interred alive in her family vault. She eventually regained consciousness, but may have died of exposure at the castle gates. The ghost has reportedly been witnessed in recent times, and is also said to haunt the Lindsay Burial Aisle in Edzell Old Churchyard.

92 miles north of Edinburgh, 33 miles north of Dundee, 42 miles south-west of Aberdeen, 7 miles north of Brechin, off B966, north of Edzell, at Edzell Castle (signposted).
NO 585693 OS: 44 DD9 7UE
Historic Scotland: open Apr-Sep, daily 9.30-17.30; last entry 30 mins before closing.
Tel: 01356 648631 Web: www.historic-scotland.gov.uk
Features: Parking. Visitor centre/shop. WC. Disabled access to garden but not into castle. Picnic area. Garden. Admission charged.
Nearest:
House of Dun (11 miles)
Dunnottar Castle (23 miles)
Glamis Castle (24 miles)
Crathes Castle (27 miles)
Drum Castle (31 miles)

EILEAN DONAN CASTLE

Colour photos page C33

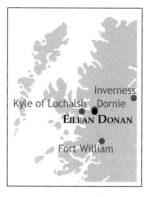

One of the most beautifully situated of all Scottish castles, Eilean Donan Castle sits on a small island in Loch Duich, reached by a bridge. The castle has a strong 13th-century wall enclosing a courtyard, with a substantial 14th-century tower of three storeys and adjoining ranges of outbuildings and fortifications, which were added in later centuries. The tower has a flush parapet, with open rounds, and the basement is barrel-vaulted, while the imposing hall is on the first floor.

Alexander III gave the lands to Colin Fitzgerald, son of the Irish Earl of Desmond and Kildare, for his help in defeating King Haakon and the Norsemen at the Battle of Largs in 1263. The family changed their name to Mackenzie, and Eilean Donan became their main stronghold. Robert the Bruce was sheltered here in 1306 during the Wars of Independence.

In 1331 Thomas Randolph, Earl of Moray, executed 50 men at Eilean Donan and adorned the castle walls with their severed heads. The castle was captured by the Earl of Huntly in 1504, and five years later the MacRaes became constables of the castle. In 1539 Eilean Donan was besieged by Donald Grumach (or Gorm) MacDonald, a claimant to the Lordship of the Isles, but he was killed by an arrow shot from the castle by one of the garrison, Duncan MacRae.

Eilean Donan Castle

103

are pierced by many gunloops. Two turnpike stairs are corbelled out above first-floor level and give access to the upper floors and the towers along with the round stair-tower.

One round tower and some walling remain from a courtyard, which formerly enclosed many buildings.

The entrance to the tower, in the re-entrant angle, leads to a wide turnpike stair and into the vaulted basement, which contains a large kitchen with an enormous fireplace, and cellars. The hall, on the first floor, has some remains of plasterwork and has a large fireplace. The lord's apartments were also on this floor. The upper floors and towers contained many more well-appointed chambers.

William Wallace is supposed to have sheltered here, but nothing of this early castle apparently remains, although the south-west tower may be older than the rest of the castle.

The Wemyss family held the property from 1468, and built the existing castle towards the end of the 16th century. They were made Lords Elcho in 1633, as well as Earls of Wemyss the same year. David, Lord Elcho, fought and survived the Battle of Culloden on the Jacobite side in 1746, but had to flee to France, where he died in 1787. He was forfeited.

By the 1780s Elcho Castle was abandoned, although it may have been used to house farm workers, and fell into decay. It was reroofed in 1830.

There is a fine quarry garden to the rear of the castle.

44 miles north of Edinburgh, 27 miles west of Dundee, 5 miles east and south of Perth, off A912, at Elcho Castle (signposted).
NO 165211 OS: 58 PH2 8QQ
Historic Scotland: open Apr-Sep, daily 9.30-17.30; last ticket sold 30 mins before closing.
Tel: 01738 639998 Web: www.historic-scotland.gov.uk
Features: Parking. Sales area. Refreshments. Picnic area. WC. Disabled access limited to exterior of property. Admission charged
Nearest:
Huntingtower (8 miles)
Scone Palace (8 miles)
Lochleven Castle (19 miles)
Drummond Castle Gardens (25 miles)
Glamis Castle (31 miles)

FALKLAND PALACE

Colour photos page C34

A fortified but comfortable residence remodelled in Renaissance style, Falkland Palace consisted of ranges of buildings around an open court. The late 15th-century gatehouse range survives complete, while an adjoining range is ruined, and only traces remain of a range opposite the gatehouse. The last side of the courtyard was completed by a wall.

The courtyard is entered through an impressive twin-towered gatehouse range, which has guardrooms on both sides of the entrance, one with a pit-prison. There are painted heraldic panels showing the arms of Scotland. The basement is vaulted, and the first floor has a large chapel, the Chapel Royal, with fine mullioned windows and a 16th-century oak screen at one end. The painted ceiling dates from 1633. There is also a fine tapestry gallery.

The ruined adjoining range once contained the king's guard hall, royal audience chamber, and private dining room, over vaulted cellars. The restored cross house contains a refurbished room, reputedly the King's Room, where James V died in 1542, as well as the Queen's Room on the first floor.

Falkland was used as a hunting seat by the kings of Scots from the 12th century. The property was owned by the MacDuff Earls of Fife in the 14th

Falkland Palace

107

Falkland Palace, bedroom

century, and the castle was destroyed by the English in 1337. It was rebuilt, and in 1371 passed to Robert Stewart, Duke of Albany. He had David, Duke of Rothesay, his nephew and the heir of Robert III, imprisoned here and starved to death, or murdered, in 1402.

After 1425, Falkland was acquired by the Crown, and it became a favourite residence of the Stewart monarchs. The palace was used and remodelled by James III, James IV, and James V, and he died at the palace in 1542.

Mary, Queen of Scots, visited the palace in 1563, James VI stayed at Falkland, as did Charles I in 1633, and Charles II in the 1650s. Despite a visit by George IV in 1822, the palace deteriorated until 1887 when it was restored by the 3rd Marquess of Bute.

The tapestry gallery is said to be haunted by a White Lady, although she has also been described as a Grey Lady. She is said to have pined away after waiting in vain for her lover to return from battle.

There are extensive gardens and the original Royal Tennis Court, dating from 1539, which is the oldest tennis court in Britain.

Falkland Palace

36 miles north of Edinburgh, 56 miles north-east of Glasgow, 22 miles south-west of Dundee, 5 miles north of Glenrothes, in the village of Falkland, on A912, at Falkland Palace (signposted).
NO 254075   OS: 59   KY15 7BU
NTS: Palace open Mar-Oct, Mon-Sat 10.00-17.00, Sun 13.00-17.00; last admission 30 mins before closing; ; outwith these times group visits by appointment; shop, also open Nov-Feb: check days and hours. Venue for weddings and events.
Tel: 0844 493 2186   Web: www.nts.org.uk
Features: Parking nearby. Shop. WC. Limited disabled access. Gardens. Real tennis court. Admission charged.
Nearest:
Hill of Tarvit (10 miles)
Lochleven Castle (13 miles)
Kellie Castle (20 miles)
St Andrews Castle (21 miles)
Aberdour Castle (23 miles)

FERNIEHIRST CASTLE

Colour photos page C35

Not far from the English border, Ferniehirst Castle is a picturesque altered and extended tower house, which incorporates the vaulted cellars from a 16th-century castle. A large stair-turret with a conical roof is decoratively corbelled out. Bartizans, with shot-holes, crown the top of the tower.

The original entrance leads to a stair known as the Left-Handed Staircase, the story being that when Sir Andrew Kerr, who was himself left-handed, returned from Flodden in 1513 he had his followers trained to use their weapons with their left hands. This is said to be the origin of the saying Corrie-fisted or Kerr-handed. The magnificent hall on the first floor has an impressive fireplace.

Ferniehirst was a property of the Kerrs, and first built around 1470, but it was taken and sacked by the English in 1523, when the Kerr laird was taken prisoner. The castle was recaptured with French help in 1549, by digging a hole through the wall. This was following years of punitive raids by the English, and the leader of the English garrison was beheaded and then hacked to pieces, while the rest of the surviving garrison was butchered with much barbarity by the Scots.

Sir Thomas Kerr, protector of Mary, Queen of Scots, invaded England in 1570, hoping to have her released, but all that resulted was a raid on Scotland, during which Ferniehirst was seized by the English and damaged. James VI attacked and partially demolished the castle in 1593, because of alleged help

Ferniehirst Castle (1909)

given by the family to Francis Stewart, the 5th Earl of Bothwell, who – among other things – was accused of using witchcraft.

The castle was rebuilt about 1598, and by marriage the family were made Marquises of Lothian in 1701. William Henry, 4th Marquis, was an aide-de-camp to the Duke of Cumberland, and he was wounded at Fontenoy, and then went on to lead the Hanoverian cavalry at the Battle of Culloden in 1746.

This branch of the Kerrs had a long-running feud with their kinsmen, the Kers of Cessford, who later built Floors Castles and became Dukes of Roxburghe.

Between 1934 and 1984 Ferniehirst was leased by the Scottish Youth Hostel Association, except during World War II when it served as an army billet. The Kerr Marquises of Lothian and Earls of Ancram still own Ferniehirst.

A Green Lady is said to haunt the castle in some tales, and unusual occurrences were reported during the time as a youth hostel, although the stories are refuted.

Another story is that a lady of the house began a series of repeated amorous liaisons with a dark stranger in the woods near the castle. In time the lady fell pregnant, but then realised that her lover was no earthly man. The lady went into labour, fearing what might be born, and a cauldron was heated over the fire to scald to death any fiend that she might bare. The ill-gotten devilish child was duly delivered but managed to evade capture and escaped up the chimney, leaving the scratches from its claws on the mantle – and these are said to still be visible.

50 miles south and east of Edinburgh, 89 miles east and south of Glasgow, 1.5 miles south of Jedburgh, on A68, Ferniehirst Castle (signposted). NT 653179 OS: 80 TD8 6UF
Open Jul, Tue-Sun 11.00-16.00 for guided tours (check with castle). Accommodation available and can be used for weddings and functions.
Tel: 07900 152986 Web: www.ferniehirst.com
Features: Parking. Gift shop. Woodland walk. Admission charged.
Nearest:
Floors Castle (15 miles)
Abbotsford (18 miles)
Mellerstain (20 miles)
Thirlestane Castle (21 miles)
Bowhill House (22 miles)

FLOORS CASTLE

Colour photos page C36

In attractive landscaped parkland with fine views and old trees and woods, Floors Castle is the largest inhabited mansion in Scotland. The magnificent building has a large towered and turreted central block with other extensive wings and ranges. The building mostly dates from 1721, and was designed by the architect William Adam for John Ker, 1st Duke of Roxburghe. This was added to the eastern end of an old tower house. In the 1830s the castle was remodelled by the architect William Playfair with a profusion of spires and domes. There is a walled garden with colourful herbaceous borders.

The old tower at Floors was burnt by the English under the Earl of Hertford in 1545. Part may be incorporated into the present mansion, and building materials were also brought from the Ker's former stronghold of Cessford (see below).

The family, now Innes-Ker, and Duke of Roxburghe, Marquis of Bowmont and Cessford, Earl of Roxburghe, Earl of Kelso, Viscount Broxmouth etc, still own Floors and manage the estate with forestry, tourism and a wind farm. Floors was used in the Tarzan film *Greystoke*.

Cessford Castle, five or so miles to the south of Floors, is an exceptionally massive ruined castle. It incorporates work from the 15th century and probably earlier, and the walls are 13 foot thick in places.

The lands were held by the Kers from the 15th century, and they soon rivalled the Ferniehirst branch of their family. Despite being kin, they got into a series of feuds, even spelling their name differently.

Floors Castle

Cessford Castle

Sir Andrew Ker of Cessford fought and survived the Battle of Flodden in 1513, and became a Warden of the Marches, although Cessford was damaged in 1519. When the Earl of Surrey besieged the castle in 1523, he reckoned Cessford was the third strongest castle in Scotland and was glad it surrendered. The castle was burnt in 1543, and damaged again by the English the following year, when the barmkin was torched.

Sir Walter Ker, also a Warden, was banished to France for his part in the murder of Walter Scott of Buccleuch in 1552 during a bloody feud with that family, and was active against Mary, Queen of Scots. The Kerrs of Ferniehirst supported her, and the two branches of the family fought on opposite sides at the Battle of Langside in 1568. The Kers of Cessford were made Earls of Roxburghe in 1616, then Dukes in 1707. The old castle was abandoned about 1650, and can be viewed from outside the crumbling walls.

35 miles south of Edinburgh, 84 miles east of Glasgow, 1 mile north-west of Kelso, off B6397, at Floors Castle (signposted).
NT 711346 OS: 74 TD5 7SF
Open Easter or Apr-end Sep, daily 10.30-17.00; end Sep-end Oct, 10.30-15.30; last entry 30 mins before closing. Venue for weddings and events. Terrace cafe and plant centre open all year (free entry).
Tel: 01573 223333 Web: www.roxburghe.net
Features: Parking. Shops. Cafes. WC. Disabled access. Walled garden. Garden centre. Grounds and walks. Adventure playground. Admission charged.
Mellerstain (7 miles)
Ferniehirst Castle (12 miles)
Abbotsford (14 miles)
Thirlestane Castle (17 miles)
Paxton House (20 miles)

FYVIE CASTLE

Colour photos page C37

Nestling in the rolling countryside of Aberdeenshire, Fyvie Castle is one of the largest and most magnificent castles in Scotland. The building consists of a massive tower house with very long wings, and is adorned with turrets, dormer windows, carved finials and corbiestepped gables.

The vaulted basement has both barrel- and groined-vaults. The fine wide main turnpike stair is decorated with 22 coats of arms. Many of the chambers are panelled in wood, and have plaster ceilings and tempera painting. The castle lies in landscaped grounds and there is an 18th-century walled garden with Scottish fruits and vegetables.

Fyvie was originally a property of the Lindsays. William the Lyon held court here in 1214, as did Alexander II in 1222. Edward I of England stayed here in 1296, during the Wars of Independence, then Robert the Bruce in 1308.

The property passed to the Prestons in 1402, then about 1433 to the Meldrums, then the Seton Earls of Dunfermline in 1596, the first of whom, Sir Alexander, was Chancellor of Scotland.

The Marquis of Montrose occupied the castle in 1644, and in the 1650s it was held by a Cromwellian force. The Setons were Jacobites and were forfeited following the Jacobite Rising of 1689-90. The property passed to the Gordon Earls of Aberdeen in 1733 and finally to the Leith family in 1889, each of whom added to the castle. It was put onto the open market in 1982, and is

Fyvie Castle

114

Fyvie Castle

now owned by The National Trust for Scotland.

Thomas the Rhymer is recorded as having made a prophecy concerning Fyvie and the Weeping Stones – this would be around the turn of the 14th century, before the Lindsays were in possession.

When the castle was first being built, stones were removed from church lands by demolishing a nearby chapel, but fell into a nearby river. The then laird refused Thomas shelter in the castle, and the Rhymer is said to have prophesied that unless the three stones were recovered the castle and estate would never descend in direct line for more than two generations. Only two of the stones were found, and the prophecy is said to have come true. One of the stones is in the charter room, while another is reported to be built into the foundations – and were said to 'weep', oozing with water, when tragedy was going to strike the owners.

The castle is reputedly haunted by several ghosts. One, the Grey Lady, is reported to be the spectre of a lady starved to death here.

Another ghost (or perhaps the same) is said to be the Green Lady, the spectre of Lilias Drummond, wife of Sir Alexander Seton, 1st Earl of Dunfermline. She died in 1601 at Dalgety in Fife, and her appearance reputedly bodes ill for the family. She may simply have died of natural causes, having given birth five times, but was perhaps starved to death by her husband, who certainly remarried quickly after her death. Lilias and Seton had had several daughters, but no sons and he wanted a male heir.

Seton remarried, and the ghost is said to have carved her name on the

Fyvie Castle, The Library

window sill of the newlyweds' bedroom in what is now called the Drummond Room, the night after they were married. The writing can still be seen: D[ame] LILLIES DRUMMOND. Her ghost is said to have been witnessed many times down the years.

152 miles north of Edinburgh, 27 miles north-west of Aberdeen, 10 miles south of Turriff, 1 mile north of Fyvie village, off A947, at Fyvie Castle (signposted).
NJ 764393   OS: 29   AB53 8JS
NTS: open Apr-Jun & Sep-Oct, Sat-Wed 12.00-17.00; Jul-Aug, daily 11.00-17.00; last entry 45 mins before closing; also Bank Hol mons; grounds and garden open all year, daily. Weddings and events.
Tel: 0844 493 2182   Web: www.nts.org.uk
Features: Parking. Gift shop. Tearoom. WC. Picnic area. Garden and grounds with lake and racquet court and bowling alley. Plant sales. Disabled access to gardens, tearoom and WC. Admission charged.
Nearest:
Haddo House (11 miles)
Delgatie Castle (12 miles)
Tolquhon Castle (13 miles)
Huntly Castle (21 miles)
Duff House (21 miles)

GLAMIS CASTLE

Colour photos page C38

One of the most famous, impressive and reputedly haunted, castles in Scotland, Glamis Castle is a magnificent grand building, consisting of a greatly extended tower dating from the 14th century. This was altered to L-plan in the 16th century, and has a large round stair-tower in the re-entrant angle. The tower was heightened, and the battlements were replaced by bartizans and dormers. The building was extended again, with lower wings and round towers, in the 17th, 18th and 19th centuries. There is extensive parkland and fine gardens.

The old tower has three vaulted storeys with very thick walls. The original kitchen was in the vaulted basement, with a huge fireplace and well. A lesser hall, also vaulted, was on the first floor, while the great hall, a fine chamber with a large fireplace and magnificent plaster ceiling, is on the second. A wide turnpike stair rises 143 steps from the basement to the battlements.

The predecessor of Glamis was reputedly intended to be built on the Hill of Denoon in the 11th century. The area was supposedly the domain of

Glamis Castle

117

GUNSGREEN HOUSE

Colour photos page C39

L ocated in the busy fishing village of Eyemouth by the harbour, Gunsgreen House was designed by the architect John Adam in the 1750s for John Nisbet, a local merchant but also a known smuggler. The house was designed to accommodate Nisbet's shady dealings. It has cavernous cellars and secret hiding places where the smuggled goods were concealed. Tea was the main contraband, and the house features a secret lead-lined tea chute, which could store up to 500 lbs of loose tea.

Nisbet went bankrupt and lost the house to his rival, Alexander Robertson. Gunsgreen was lived in by many families over the years, before becoming a popular guest house and later the town golf club. The house was restored by the Gunsgreen House Trust and was opened to the public in 2009.

52 miles east of Edinburgh, 8 miles north of Berwick-upon-Tweed, in Eyemouth by harbour, along The Avenue, at Gunsgreen House (signposted).
NT 948644   OS: 67   TD14 5SD
Open Apr-Oct, Thu-Mon 11.00-17.00, last admission 16.15; groups at other times by appt and check winter. Venue for weddings and events. Luxury self-catering accommodation available.
Tel: 018907 52062   Web: www.gunsgreenhouse.org
Parking. Shop. WC. Disabled access. Exhibitions. Admission charged. Refreshments, ice cream and much else in Eyemouth.
Paxton House (10 miles)
Manderston (13 miles)
Mellerstain (30 miles)
Floors Castle (33 miles)
Thirlestane Castle (33 miles)

HADDO HOUSE

Colour photo page C40

Haddo House is an impressive although somewhat plain classical mansion of 1731-6 with two sweeping wings. The house was built for William Gordon, 2nd Earl of Aberdeen, by the architect William Adam. It was remodelled in the 1880s. The house replaced a castle of the Gordons, who had held the lands from 1429, but nothing survives of this old stronghold.

Patrick Gordon of Haddo was killed at the Battle of Arbroath in 1446, and the family had an aisle at Tarves. In 1644 Sir John Gordon of Haddo, who had been active with the Marquis of Montrose, was captured after being besieged in the castle for three days. He was imprisoned in Haddo's Hole in St Giles Cathedral before being executed by beheading. The castle was destroyed.

His son, Sir George, however, became Lord Chancellor of Scotland and Earl of Aberdeen in 1684, while George, 4th Earl, was Prime Minister of Great Britain, although he resigned in 1854.

John, 7th Earl, was made Marquess of Aberdeen and Temair in 1915 after being Lord Lieutenant of Ireland and Governor General of Canada.

Haddo House

Haddo House, Library

The Premier's Bedroom is reputed to be haunted by the ghost of Lord Archibald Gordon, who was a son of the Marquess of Aberdeen and was killed in 1909 in one of the first car accidents in Britain.

There is a fine terraced garden and adjacent country park, with walks, lakes and monuments.

146 miles north of Edinburgh, 20 miles north and west of Aberdeen, 8 miles north-west of Ellon, 7 miles north-east of Old Meldrum, off B999, at Haddo House (signposted).
NJ 868347   OS: 30   AB41 7EQ
NTS: open Apr-Jun & Sep-late Oct, Fri-Mon; Jul-Aug, daily – guided tours at 11.30, 13.30 and 15.30 (booking is recommended and tel to check opening); shop and tearoom, open Apr-late Oct, daily; Oct-early Apr, Sat & Sun only; grounds and garden open all year, daily 9.00-sunset.
Tel: 0844 493 2179   Web: www.nts.org.uk
Features: Parking. Gift shop. Tearoom. WC. Garden. Adjoining country park. Disabled access. Admission charged.
Nearest:
Tolquhon Castle (5 miles)
Fyvie Castle (11 miles)
Delgatie Castle (19 miles)
Castle Fraser (20 miles)
Huntly Castle (28 miles)

HERMITAGE CASTLE

Colour photo page C40

Glasgow   Edinburgh

HERMITAGE

Dumfries
Newcastleton

One of the most impressive and oppressive of Scottish fortresses, Hermitage Castle consists of a 13th-century courtyard and large 14th-century tower of four storeys, around which has been constructed a massively strong castle. The tower had small square towers added at three of the corners, and the entrance was at first-floor level and defended by two portcullises. In the 15th century a new rectangular wing was extended from the main tower. The castle lies in a bare and windswept location, not far from the border with England.

The walls are pierced by small windows and splayed gunloops. A timber gallery projected around the whole building, the holes to support the joists still visible.

The property belonged to the Dacres, who had a castle here in the 13th

Hermitage Castle

123

century, but passed to the Soulis family, who strengthened Hermitage. One of the family (probably William or possibly Sir Richard, his father) was said to be a man of ill repute and to dabble in witchcraft. Many local children were reputedly seized by Soulis and never seen again, their corpses to be used in his diabolic conjurings. Soulis could not be killed by ordinary means. The local people, according to one story, eventually rebelled and Soulis was wrapped in lead and boiled in a cauldron at the nearby stone circle of Nine Stane Rig, although he may actually have been imprisoned in Dumbarton Castle for supporting the English. Whatever the truth of it, the family were forfeited in 1320.

The castle passed to the Grahams of Abercorn, then by marriage to the Douglas family. William Douglas, the Knight of Liddesdale, was prominent in resisting Edward Balliol in the 1330s and recovered Hermitage from the English. In a dispute over who had been given the Sheriffdom of Teviotdale, Douglas seized Sir Alexander Ramsay of Dalhousie, while the latter was at his devotions in St Mary's Church at Hawick. Ramsay was imprisoned in a dungeon at the castle and starved to death. In 1353, however, Douglas was murdered by his own godson, another William Douglas, after he had tried to block his claim to the lordship of Douglas.

In 1492 Archibald, 5th Earl of Angus, exchanged Hermitage for Bothwell with Patrick Hepburn, Earl of Bothwell. In 1566 James Hepburn, 4th Earl of Bothwell, was badly wounded by the Border reiver Little Jock Elliot of Park Little Jock was shot and eventually died (or, perhaps, survived until 1590…), but Bothwell was paid a visit on his sick bed by Mary, Queen of Scots.

The castle and title passed by forfeiture to Francis Stewart, Earl of Bothwell, then after he was forfeited to the Scotts of Buccleuch.

The are the remains of a chapel and burial ground to the west of the castle.

Ghostly screams and cries can sometimes reputedly be heard from the victims of Lord Soulis around Hermitage, and his own ghost has been reported here. The ghost of Alexander Ramsay is said to have been witnessed within the walls, as has that of Mary, Queen of Scots, clad in a white dress, outside the castle.

One story is that so much wickedness had been perpetrated at Hermitage that it had sunk into the ground, although artillery fortifications might be a more prosaic explanation for the mounds round the castle…

66 miles south of Edinburgh, 49 miles east and north of Dumfries, 6 miles north of Newcastleton, off B6357, at Hermitage Castle (signposted).
NY 494960 OS: 79 TD9 0LU
Historic Scotland: open Apr-Sep, daily 9.30-17.30, last entry 30 mins before closing.
Tel: 01387 376222 Web: www.historic-scotland.gov.uk
Features: Parking. Sales area. Admission charged.
Ferniehirst Castle (22 miles)
Bowhill House (30 miles)
Floors Castle (39 miles)
Mellerstain (41 miles)
Traquair House (43 miles)

HILL OF TARVIT

Colour photos page C41

Embosomed by 273 acres of gardens, woodland and grounds, Hill of Tarvit is an elegant two-storey symmetrical mansion with small projecting bow-fronted wings. The original house dating from 1696 was designed by the architect Sir William Bruce for the Wemyss family (who changed the name to Wemyss House) and was given wings in the 19th century. It was then virtually rebuilt in 1906 by the architect Sir Robert Lorimer for Frederick B. Sharp, a Dundee industrialist. Sharp wanted to house

Hill of Tarvit

his fine collections of paintings and pictures, including by Raeburn and Ramsay, furniture, Flemish tapestries and Chinese porcelain and bronzes. There are fine formal gardens, also designed by Lorimer, as well as a walled garden.

Close to Hill of Tarvit, Scotstarvit Tower is a well-preserved, tall and impressive tower house, dating from the 15th and 16th century. It has a corbelled-out parapet without rounds, with fabulous views from the battlements, and the walls are pierced by shot-holes. The small stair-wing is crowned by a caphouse with a conical roof.

Hill of Tarvit

The arched entrance, in the re-entrant angle, leads through a lobby to the vaulted basement and to the turnpike stair, in the wing, which climbs to all floors. The basement has had an entresol. The hall, on the first floor, has a moulded fireplace and windows with stone seats. The storey above this is also vaulted. A fireplace from the attic, dating from 1627, was reset in the Smoking Room at Hill of Tarvit.

Scotstarvit was originally a property of the Inglis family, but was sold to the Scotts in 1611. Sir John Scott of Scotstarvit was Director of the Chancellory, geographer, writer and an eminent historian. He was author of *Scot of Scotstarvet's Staggering State of the Scots Statesmen*. The property was sold to the Gourlays of Craigrothie about 1780, then to the owners of Hill of Tarvit.

42 miles north of Edinburgh, 16 miles south of Dundee, 3 miles south of Cupar, off A916, at Hill of Tarvit (signposted).
NO 380119   OS: 59   KY15 5PB
NTS: open Apr-late Oct, Thu-Mon 13.00-17.00, last entry 45 mins before closing; garden and grounds open all year, closing at dusk.
Tel: 0844 493 2185   Web: www.nts.org.uk
Features: Parking. Shop. Tearoom (also open when sign displayed). WC. Plant sales. Gardens and grounds. Disabled access to ground floor of house, shop and tearoom. Admission charged.
Scotstarvit Tower. Key available at Hill of Tarvit (see that entry) or from cottage by tower. Park in lay-by by A916 (opposite entrance to Hill of Tarvit).

Nearest:
Falkland Palace (10 miles)
St Andrews Castle (10 miles)
Kellie Castle (12 miles)
Lochleven Castle (23 miles)
Glamis Castle (28 miles)

Scotstarvit Tower

HOPETOUN HOUSE

Colour photos page C42

South Queensferry
HOPETOUN
Glasgow Edinburgh

Situated on the shores of the Firth of Forth and at the centre of a 6,500 acre estate, Hopetoun House is a large, imposing and stately palatial mansion. The house has a long classical central block of four storeys and sweeping flanking wings. The oldest part of the house dates from 1699-1707, and was designed by the architect Sir William Bruce for the Hope family.

The family are descended from the Hopes of Craighall, which was a property in Fife. Sir Charles Hope, Lord Lieutenant of Linlithgow and Governor of the Bank of Scotland, was made Earl of Hopetoun in 1703. He had the house enlarged and remodelled by the architect William Adam from 1721, the work being continued by John and Robert Adam. In 1902 John Hope, 7th Earl of Hopetoun, who also served as Governor General of Australia and Secretary of State for Scotland, was made Marquess of Linlithgow. Hopetoun was transferred to a charitable trust in 1974, although the Earls of Hopetoun still live at the house.

There are fine interiors, dating from the late Georgian period through to the Edwardian, and the house is set in 100 acres of gardens and rolling park land.

Hopetoun House

Hopetoun House, Stair

13 miles west of Edinburgh, 43 miles east of Glasgow, 2.5 miles west of South Queensferry, off A904, at Hopetoun House (signposted).
NT 089790   OS: 65   EH30 9SL* *do not use for SatNav
Open Apr (or earlier depending on Easter)-last Sun in Sep 10.30-17.00; last entry 60 mins before closing; other times closed except for group visits by prior appt. Venue for weddings and events. Holiday accommodation.
Tel: 0131 331 2451   Web: www.hopetoun.co.uk
Features: Parking. Shop. Farm shop. Tearoom. WC. Disabled access to house main floor. Gardens and grounds. Admission charged.
Nearest:
The Binns (8 miles)
Blackness Castle (9 miles (by road))
Lauriston Castle (10 miles)
Linlithgow Palace (11 miles)
Aberdour Castle (12 miles)

HOUSE OF DUN

Colour photo page C43

House of Dun is a fine classical mansion, built in 1730 by the architect William Adam for David Erskine, Lord Dun, a judge of the Court of Session. The house has good plasterwork, and is home to the NTS Hutchison and Stirling collections, some of the finest paintings and furniture owned by the Trust.

There are formal gardens with hundreds of acres of woodland and parkland, as well as a 19th-century walled garden.

The house replaced an ancient castle, little of which survives except one arch, about 400 yards west of the present mansion.

The lands were held by the Hastings family in the 12th and 13th centuries, and John Hastings was Lord of Dun and Sheriff and Forester of the Mearns. The property had gone to the Erskines by 1375. One of the family was John Erskine of Dun, a scholar and reformer in the time of Mary, Queen of Scots.

The castle was the scene of a notorious case of poisoning, reputed witchcraft and murder in 1613, when the young John Erskine, heir to Dun, and his brother Alexander were poisoned by Robert Erskine, his uncle, and his three aunts in a dispute over property. The older boy died in agony, while Alexander survived after a severe illness, and eventually succeeded to the lands. Robert Erskine and two of his sisters were executed, while the third had to go into exile.

The Erskines held the property until 1980, at which time the house was being used as a hotel, when it passed to The National Trust for Scotland.

House of Dun

130

House of Dun

The house and estate is said to be haunted by three or more apparitions, including a harpist who plays in the Den of Dun, a headless huntsman seen in the grounds around the house, and a White Lady.

90 miles north and east of Edinburgh, 32 miles north-east of Dundee, 4 miles west of Montrose, off A935, at House of Dun (signposted). NO 667599 OS: 54 DD10 9LQ
NTS: House open for guided tours: Easter-Jun and Sep-late Oct, Wed-Sun 12.30-17.30; Jul-Aug, daily 11.30-17.30; last entry 45 mins before closing; also Bank Hol Mons in the summer; garden and grounds open all year, daily 9.30-sunset.
Tel: 0844 493 2144 Web: www.nts.org.uk
Features: Parking. Gift shop. Restaurant. Model theatres. Adventure playground. Walled garden. Woodland walk. Disabled access to ground floor and basement and WC. Admission charged.
Nearest:
Edzell Castle (11 miles)
Dunnottar Castle (23 miles)
Glamis Castle (24 miles)
Crathes Castle (33 miles)
St Andrews Castle (44 miles)

HUNTINGTOWER

Colour photo page C43

A stark and striking castle, Huntingtower has three different phases of building. The oldest part is a 15th-century tower of three storeys and a garret, rectangular in plan. Nearby, but not touching, a 16th-century L-plan tower house was built, consisting of a main block of four storeys and a wing rising a storey higher. The only communication between these was a wooden bridge. Towards the end of the 16th century, a connecting range of three storeys was added, containing a stair for both towers.

The hall of the L-plan tower has a fine painted ceiling and beams, and there are also remains of mural paintings and plasterwork.

The property was held by the Ruthvens from the 12th century, and was originally called Ruthven Castle. The Ruthvens fought against the English during the Wars of Independence, and they were made Sheriffs of Perth in 1313, and then Lords Ruthven in 1488. William, Master of Ruthven, was killed at the Battle of Flodden in 1513. Mary, Queen of Scots, visited the castle in 1565 while on honeymoon with Darnley, although the 3rd Lord Ruthven, Patrick, took part in the murder of Rizzio, Mary's secretary.

In 1582 William, 4th Lord Ruthven, who had been made Earl of Gowrie the previous year, kidnapped the young James VI – in what became known as the Raid of Ruthven – and held him in Huntingtower for a year until the King escaped during a hunting trip. The Earl was beheaded in 1585.

Huntingtower

Huntingtower, painted ceiling

In 1600 John Ruthven, 3rd Earl of Gowrie and his brother, Alexander, Master of Ruthven, were slain in Gowrie House in Perth by James VI and his followers, following the Gowrie Conspiracy, a possible plot to murder the king – or at least to kidnap him. The Ruthvens were forfeited, their lands seized, and their name proscribed.

The property passed to the Marquises of Atholl in 1676. Lord George Murray, Bonnie Prince Charlie's general in the 1745-6 Jacobite Rising, was born here. Huntingtower was later used to house labourers in the calico printing industry.

The space between the battlements of the two towers is known as The Maiden's Leap. Dorothy, daughter of the 1st Earl of Gowrie, is supposed to have leapt from one tower to the other after visiting her lover.

The castle and grounds are said to be haunted by a Green Lady. Her footsteps have reputedly been heard, along with the rustle of her gown.

44 miles north of Edinburgh, 3 miles north-west of Perth, off A85 west of junction with A9, at Huntingtower (signposted).
NO 083252 OS: 58 PH1 3JL
Historic Scotland: open Apr-Sep, daily 9.30-17.30; Oct-Mar, Sat-Wed 9.30-16.30; closed 25/26 Dec and 1/2 Jan; last ticket sold 30 mins before closing.
Tel: 01738 627231 Web: www.historic-scotland.gov.uk
Features: Parking. Gift shop. Refreshments. WC. Limited disabled access. Picnic area. Garden. Admission charged.
Nearest:
Scone Palace (5 miles)
Elcho Castle (8 miles)
Drummond Castle Gardens (19 miles)
Lochleven Castle (20 miles)
Glamis Castle (28 miles)

HUNTLY CASTLE

Colour photo page C44

A grand building with a long and violent history, Huntly Castle consists of a strong 15th-century tower, rectangular in plan, with a large round tower at one end and a smaller circular tower at the opposite corner. The upper storey of the tower was remodelled in the late 16th century with decorative stonework, inscribed friezes and new windows, including three oriels. An adjoining large courtyard had ranges of buildings on two sides, and nothing remains of an older tower except foundations.

From the entrance to the castle, a straight stair leads down to the vaulted basement, which contains three cellars and a prison in the large round tower. The floor above, at ground level, is also vaulted and contains two cellars and a

Huntly Castle

Huntly Castle, oriel windows

kitchen, with a private chamber in the round tower. The hall, on the main first floor, was a fine chamber, but was later subdivided, and there are magnificent carved decorative fireplaces.

The property was called Strathbogie, but passed to the Gordons early in the 14th century. Robert the Bruce stayed here before defeating the Comyn Earl of Buchan at a battle nearby in 1307.

An older castle was burned down in 1452 by the Earl of Moray. The Gordons were made Earls of Huntly in 1455, and Alexander, first Earl and Chancellor of Scotland, was buried in St Mary's Aisle of Elgin Cathedral, his stone effigy surviving, although headless and defaced. In 1496 Perkin Warbeck, a pretender to the English throne, married Catherine Gordon here in the presence of James IV. In 1506 the name was changed from Strathbogie to Huntly, from a property of that name near Gordon in the Borders. Alexander Gordon, 3rd Earl, led the left flank of the Scottish forces at the Battle of Flodden in 1513, but managed to escape alive.

George, 4th Earl, was defeated (and died, reportedly from apoplexy) by the forces of Mary, Queen of Scots, at the Battle of Corrichie in 1562, and his son, Sir John, was executed. The castle was slighted and pillaged at this time, the treasure from St Machar's Cathedral in Aberdeen being seized. George, 5th Earl, was accused of treason and forfeited in 1563, but this was reversed two years later, and he was Chancellor from 1566-7. The 6th Earl, another George, led a rising against James VI and defeated forces under the Earl of Argyll at the Battle of Glenlivet in 1594. Despite this victory, Huntly Castle was attacked by James VI and damaged, to be restored once again in 1602. The Earl had been pardoned and then made Marquis of Huntly in 1599.

In 1640 the castle was occupied by a Covenanting army, who destroyed much of the interior. In 1644 it was taken by forces of the Marquis of Montrose, but it was captured by General David Leslie three years later after starving out and slaughtering the garrison. George, 2nd Marquis of Huntly, was hanged for

135

Huntly Castle, Marchioness's Lodging fireplace

his support of Charles I in 1649. George, 4th Marquis, was made Duke of Gordon in 1684, although this title became extinct in 1836.

The castle was garrisoned by Hanoverian soldiers during the Jacobite Rising of 1745-6, but by then had been abandoned as a residence, although it was still roofed in 1799. It was then used as a quarry and dump until cleared in 1923.

144 miles north of Edinburgh, 39 miles north-west of Aberdeen, 66 miles east of Inverness, to the north of Huntly, off A920 in Huntly, at Huntly Castle (signposted).
NJ 532407   OS: 29   AB54 4SH
Historic Scotland: open Apr-Sep, daily 9.30-17.30; Oct-Mar, Sat-Wed 9.30-16.30, closed Thu & Fri; last ticket sold 30 mins before closing; closed 25/26 Dec and 1/2 Jan.
Tel: 01466 793191   Web: www.historic-scotland.gov.uk
Features: Parking. Gift shop. WC. Disabled WC. Admission charged.
Nearest:
Balvenie Castle (15 miles)
Kildrummy Castle (17 miles)
Delgatie Castle (20 miles)
Duff House (21 miles)
Fyvie Castle (22 miles)

INVERARAY CASTLE

Colour photos page C45

I n a lovely position by the banks of the sinuous Loch Fyne at the mouth of the Aray river, Inveraray Castle is an imposing and iconic castellated mansion, home of the Campbells of Argyll for hundreds of years. The present castle was begun in 1746, and was designed by the architects Roger Morris and William Adam, then completed by John and Robert Adam, not being finished until 43 years after the first stone was laid. The castle suffered a fire in 1877, and was then restored with the addition of a third floor and conical roofs on the corner towers.

The castle houses many interesting rooms, with collections of tapestries and paintings, and superb displays of weapons. Rob Roy MacGregor's sporran and dirk handle are on display. Near the present castle is the site of the old tower, which rose to four storeys with bartizans. The old tower was demolished as part of Archibald, 3rd Duke of Argyll's, rebuilding of a new castle and town.

Inveraray was long a property of the Campbells, and Colin Campbell, 1st Earl of Argyll, was Lord High Chancellor of Scotland in 1483. Archibald, 2nd Earl, was slain at the Battle of Flodden in 1513, and the 4th Earl, another Archibald, was at the forefront of the Reformation. James V visited the old castle in 1533, as did Mary, Queen of Scots, thirty years later. Archibald, 5th Earl, led Mary's forces to defeat at the Battle of Langside in 1568, and was later Lord High Chancellor of Scotland.

Archibald, 8th Earl, was made Marquis of Argyll in 1641. He led the forces

Inveraray Castle

Inveraray Castle, Armoury Hall

that were defeated by the Marquis of Montrose at Inverlochy and Kilsyth in 1645, and the castle had been pillaged and burnt the previous year by Montrose. Montrose was finally defeated later that year, but the Earl cooperated with the Cromwellian administration and was himself executed by beheading using the Maiden in 1661 after the Restoration of Charles II. Archibald, 9th Earl, was found guilty of treason and then later led an invasion of Scotland in 1685, but this failed and he was also beheaded. Archibald, 10th Earl, was made Duke of Argyll in 1701, while, John, 2nd Duke, led the Hanoverian forces at the Battle of Sheriffmuir in 1715. The castle is still owned by the Dukes of Argyll.

65 miles north-west of Glasgow, 108 miles west of Edinburgh, 38 miles east and south of Oban, north of Inveraray village, off A83, at Inveraray Castle (signposted).
NN 096093 OS: 56 PA32 8XE
Open Apr-Oct, daily 10.00-17.45, last admission 17.00. Venue for events and weddings. Holiday cottages and park.
Tel: 01499 302203 Web: www.inveraray-castle.com
Features: Parking. Gift shop. Tea room. WC. Garden and woodland walks. Disabled access to ground floor only. Admission charged.
Kilchurn Castle (15 miles)
Carnasserie Castle (24 miles)
Dunstaffnage Castle (36 miles)
Skipness Castle (51 miles)
Rothesay Castle, Bute (52 miles (ferry))

KELLIE CASTLE

Colour photo page C44

O ne of the finest castles in Scotland,
Kellie Castle is a 16th- and 17th-
century E-plan tower house. There is
a three-storey main block with three large square
towers, which form the E. The towers rise to
five storeys, and two have bartizans. Two smaller
stair-towers project from one side. The oldest part
of the castle, one of the towers, dates from the
early 16th century (or perhaps from 1360); another tower was added in 1573.
The main block and a large tower were added to connect the older parts of the
building in 1603-6.

The basement is vaulted throughout the building. A square stair rises, from
the main entrance, to the large hall on the first floor. Four turnpike stairs also
climb to hall level. The Vine Room, on one of the upper floors, has a ceiling
painted by De Witt, and there are also fine plaster ceilings. A mural by the arts-
and-crafts pioneer Phoebe Traquair was long hidden.

There is a magnificent walled garden featuring a good collection of old

Kellie Castle

fashioned roses and herbaceous plants which are organically cultivated.

An earlier castle here belonged to the Siwards, but the present castle was built by the Oliphants, who held the lands from 1360 until 1613, when Laurence, 5th Lord Oliphant, had to sell the property. It was bought by Sir Thomas Erskine of Gogar, made Earl of Kellie in 1619, a favourite of James VI. Erskine was involved in the Gowrie Conspiracy in 1601, and may have been one of those who slew the Master of Ruthven and his brother, the Earl of Gowrie, at Gowrie House in Perth. Alexander Erskine, 5th Earl of Kellie, was a Jacobite, and had to hide in the stump of a tree for the summer following the Battle of Culloden in 1746.

Kellie was abandoned in 1829, but in 1878 James Lorimer, Professor of Public Law at Edinburgh University, leased Kellie as an almost roofless ruin and proceeded to restore it. Robert Lorimer, his son, spent most of his childhood at Kellie, and was later a famous architect.

A turnpike stair in the castle is reputedly haunted by the spirit of Anne Erskine, who died by falling from one of the upstairs windows. The ghost of James Lorimer is also said to have been seen seated in one of the passageways.

45 miles north-east of Edinburgh, 23 miles south of Dundee, 4 miles north and west of Anstruther, off B9171, at Kellie Castle (signposted).
NO 520052   OS: 59   KY10 2RF
NTS: Castle open Apr-May, Thu-Mon 12.30-17.00; Jun-Aug, daily 12.30-17.00; Sep, Thu-Mon 12.30-17.00; Oct, Thu-Mon, 12.30-16.00; groups by arrangement outwith these times; garden and estate, open all year except 25-26 Dec & 1-2 Jan, daily 9.30-18.00 or dusk if earlier.
Tel: 08444 493 2184   Web: www.nts.org.uk
Features: Parking. Gift shop. Cafe (open earlier than castle). WC. Plant sales. Walled garden. Woodland walks. Disabled access to ground floor of castle, shop, tearoom and garden. Admission charged.
Nearest:
St Andrews Castle (11 miles)
Hill of Tarvit (12 miles)
Falkland Palace (21 miles)
Lochleven Castle (31 miles)
Aberdour Castle (32 miles)

KILCHURN CASTLE

Colour photo page C46

A picturesque and much photographed ruin on a peninsula (a former island) in Loch Awe, Kilchurn Castle is a courtyard castle of the 15th century. The castle has a rectangular tower of four storeys and a garret, which was extended with ranges of buildings in the 16th and 17th centuries. It is located in one of the most scenic parts of Scotland, dominated by the dramatic mountain of Ben Cruachan.

The basement of the tower is vaulted, and contained the kitchen. The hall, on the first floor, only had a small fireplace. The floors above are gone. There are excellent views from the top of the tower (on a clear day).

The courtyard has round towers at the corners, which are pierced by shot-holes. The other ranges are late 17th-century barrack-blocks, and there are two large kitchen fireplaces.

The lands originally belonged to the MacGregors, but were acquired by the Campbells of Glenorchy, who built the castle, although probably on the site of an earlier stronghold. The castle was strengthened and improved by Black Duncan of the Seven Castles, Sir Duncan Campbell, at the end of the 16th century, after damage inflicted by the MacGregors. The Campbells withstood a two-day siege in 1654 by the Royalist General Middleton before he retreated from Monck's Cromwellian forces.

Sir John Campbell of Glenorchy acquired the extensive lands of George

Kilchurn Castle

Kilchurn Castle

Sinclair, 6th Earl of Caithness, by foreclosing on his vast debts, and even claimed the title of Earl. He led a bloody campaign in the north in 1680, and reportedly slew so many Sinclairs that the Campbells crossed the Wick River without getting their feet wet. This was when the song 'The Campbells are Coming' was composed. Although he failed to hold the Earldom of Caithness, he was made Earl of Breadalbane instead.

The castle was used by the Campbells until 1740 when they moved to Balloch, which is now called Taymouth. Kilchurn was garrisoned by Hanoverian troops in 1745 but was unroofed by 1775.

Contender for the midgiest place in the world on a grey airless day in July.

99 miles west and north of Edinburgh, 76 miles north-west of Glasgow, 2 miles west of Dalmally, off A85 west of junction with A819, at Kilchurn Castle (not signposted).
NN 133276 OS: 50 PA33 1AF
Historic Scotland: open Apr-Sep: parking access from A85, then walk under nearby railway viaduct to castle. Can be muddy and may flood.
Tel: 01866 833333 Web: www.historic-scotland.gov.uk
Features: Parking nearby. 0.5 miles walk to castle.
Inveraray Castle (15 miles)
Dunstaffnage Castle (21 miles)
Carnasserie Castle (31 miles)
Skipness Castle (65 miles)
Rothesay Castle, Bute (65 miles (ferry))

Abbotsford

Aberdour Castle

Ballindalloch Castle

Ballindalloch Castle, Dining Room

Balvenie Castle

Blackness Castle

Blair Castle

Blair Castle, Picture Staircase

Bothwell
Castle

Brodick Castle

Bowhill House

Bowhill House, Dining Room

Braemar Castle

Braemar Castle, Dining Room

Brodie Castle

Caerlaverock Castle

Callendar House

Callendar House, Kitchen

Cardoness Castle

Carnasserie Castle

Castle Campbell

Castle Fraser

Castle Menzies

Castle Menzies, Hall

Castle of Mey

Cawdor Castle

Craigievar Castle

Craigievar Castle, Hall

C14

Craigmillar Castle

Craignethan Castle

Crathes
Castle

Crathes Castle, Room of the Nine Nobles

Crichton Castle

Culross Palace

Culzean
Castle

Culzean Castle, Oval Stair

Delgatie
Castle

Delgatie Castle, painted ceiling

Dean Castle

Dirleton Castle

Doune Castle

Drum Castle

Drumlanrig Castle

Drumlanrig Castle, Drawing Room

Drumlanrig
Castle

Drumlanrig Castle

Drummond Castle Gardens

Drummond Castle Gardens

Duart Castle

Duart Castle

Dumfries House

Dumfries House,
Pewter Corridor

Dunnottar
Castle

Dunnottar Castle

Dunrobin
Castle

Dunrobin Castle, Drawing Room

Duff House

Dunstaffnage Castle

Dunvegan Castle

Edinburgh Castle

Edinburgh Castle, St Margaret's Chapel

Edinburgh Castle, Mons Meg

Edzell Castle

Elcho Castle

C32

Eilean Donan Castle

Eilean Donan Castle

Falkland Palace

Falkland Palace, tapestry in the Chapel Royal

Ferniehirst Castle

Ferniehirst Castle, Hall

Glamis Castle

Glamis Castle, Duncan's Hall

Gunsgreen House

Gunsgreen House, blue panelled room

Haddo House

Hermitage Castle

Hill of Tarvit

Hill of Tarvit, Dining Hall

Hopetoun House

Hopetoun House

Hopetoun House, Red Drawing Room

House of Dun

Huntingtower Castle

Huntly Castle

Kellie Castle

Inveraray
Castle

Inveraray Castle, State Dining Room

Kilchurn Castle

Kildrummy Castle

Lauriston Castle

Lochleven Castle

Linlithgow
Palace

Linlithgow Palace, courtyard and fountain

Manderston

Manderston

Mellerstain

Mellerstain, Library

Mellerstain, Library ceiling

Mellerstain, Rose Garden looking south

Mount Stuart

Mount Stuart, Marble Hall

Mount Stuart, Horoscope Room

Mount Stuart

Newark Castle

Newhailes

Palace of Holyroodhouse

Pollok House

Paxton House

Paxton House, Entrance Hall

C56

Rothesay Castle

Scone Palace

Skipness Castle

Spynie Palace

St Andrews Castle

The Binns

Stirling Castle

Stirling Castle, Great Hall

Tantallon Castle

Tantallon Castle

Thirlestane Castle

Threave Castle

Tolquhon
Castle

Tolquhon Castle

Traquair House

Traquair House, Drawing Room

KILDRUMMY CASTLE

Colour photo page C46

A lthough now quite ruinous, Kildrummy Castle, built in the 13th century, was one of the largest and mightiest early castles in Scotland, and remains a fine pile in a picturesque setting. The high curtain walls enclosed a courtyard with six round towers at the corners and a gate. One of these, the largest, called The Snow Tower, may have been the main donjon, and was similar to that at Coucy.

The gatehouse is much reduced, but was formerly defended by two towers, and resembles Edward I's castle of Harlech. Nearby was the two-storey hall block, the walls of which are the best preserved part of the castle. There was also a chapel, three tall lancet windows of which remain.

Kildrummy was captured by Edward I of England in 1296, and then again in 1306 from a garrison led by Nigel, younger brother of Robert the Bruce, after the castle was set alight by a traitor. Nigel, and the rest of the garrison, were executed by hanging. The traitor was rewarded with much gold – poured molten down his throat.

The castle was restored before 1333, and besieged by the Earl of Atholl acting for the English in 1335. It was successfully defended by Bruce's sister, Christian. Her husband, Sir Andrew Moray, the Regent, relieved the castle and killed the Earl of Atholl at or after the Battle of Culbean. David II besieged the castle in 1363, and seized it from the Earl of Mar.

Kildrummy Castle

Kildrummy Castle

Kildrummy was in royal hands from 1361–8, until Alexander Stewart, son of the Wolf of Badenoch, acquired it after he had forced Isabella Douglas, Countess of Mar, to marry him in 1404. He may have had the poor women's husband, Sir Malcolm Drummond, killed. Stewart's son led the king's forces at the Battle of Harlaw in 1411. The castle was sacked and torched in 1530 by John Strachan of Lynturk, and was captured in 1654 by Cromwell's forces.

The castle was badly damaged in 1690, when it was burned by Jacobites, but was complete enough for the Earl of Mar to use it as his base when he led the Jacobite Rising in 1715. After the collapse of the Jacobite cause, Kildrummy was deliberately dismantled and used as a quarry.

There are fine gardens nearby at Kildrummy Castle Gardens.

127 miles north of Edinburgh, 35 miles west of Aberdeen, 10 miles west of Alford, 1 mile south-west of hamlet of Kildrummy, off A97, at Kildrummy Castle (signposted).
NJ 454164   OS: 37   AB33 8RA
Historic Scotland: open Apr-Sep, daily 9.30-17.30; last entry 30 mins before closing.
Tel: 01975 571331   Web: www.historic-scotland.gov.uk
Features: Parking. Gift shop. Refreshments. WC. Disabled WC. Admission charged.
Kildrummy Castle Gardens open Apr-Oct
Tel: 01975 571203   Web: www.kildrummy-castle-gardens.co.uk
Nearest:
Craigievar Castle (14 miles)
Castle Fraser (21 miles)
Crathes Castle (32 miles)
Drum Castle (32 miles)
Braemar Castle (35 miles)

LAURISTON CASTLE

Colour photo page C47

LAURISTON
Glasgow   Edinburgh

In wooded policies looking out over the Firth of Forth and Cramond Inch, Lauriston Castle is a romantic castle and mansion. A tower house of three storeys and an attic, dating from the 16th century, was extended by a two-storey Jacobean-style extension, designed by the architect William Burn in 1824-7. The tower has a round stair-tower, and two large pepperpot turrets, as well as very tall chimneys. Lauriston stands in fine grounds and gardens, which were laid out by William Playfair in the 1840s, and there is a Japanese Friendship Garden, gifted by the people of Kyoto.

The basement of the old part is vaulted and the hall, on the first floor, has a hidden stair leading to a spy hole. The castle has a fine Edwardian-period interior with Italian furniture, Sheffield plate and Blue John ornaments.

The lands were held by the Forresters, but the castle was built by the Napiers of Merchiston. One of the family, John Napier, was the inventor of logarithms. In 1656 the property was sold to Charles II's solicitor, Robert Dalgleish, then went though several other families before coming to the Reids, owners of Morrison & Co, a leading Edinburgh cabinet-making business. They were the last owners, and gave the castle to the nation in 1926.

Lauriston Castle

145

Lauriston Castle

3 miles west & north of Edinburgh Castle, between Davidson's Mains and Cramond, Cramond Road South, at Lauriston Castle (signposted). NT 204762 OS: 66 EH4 5QD
Open Mar-Oct, Sat-Thu for guided tour at 14.00, closed Fri; Nov-Mar, Sat & Sun 14.00 only, closed Mon-Fri; group visits by appt at other times; gardens open Apr-Sep, daily 9.00-20.00; Oct-Mar, daily 9.00-17.00. Events programme. Venue hire.
Tel: 0131 336 2060 Web: www.edinburghmuseums.org.uk
Features: Parking. Sales area. Japanese Friendship Garden. No disabled access to castle. Admission charged to castle; garden free.
Edinburgh Castle (3 miles)
Palace of Holyroodhouse (5 miles)
Craigmillar Castle (8 miles)
Hopetoun House (10 miles)
The Binns (12 miles)

LINLITHGOW PALACE

Colour photos page C48

Once a splendid edifice and still a spectacular ruin in a picturesque spot by the loch, Linlithgow Palace consists of ranges of buildings set around a rectangular courtyard, and may include 12th-century work. Stair-towers, within the courtyard, lead to all floors and to the battlements, which run all round. The hall has been a magnificent chamber with an unusual tripartite fireplace, as has been the chapel, and there are many other rooms in this stately building.

There is a fine carved fountain in the courtyard, dating from 1538, which has recently been restored to working order.

The main entrance was originally to the east and dates from the 15th century, but this was moved to the south in the 16th century. The north range collapsed at the beginning of the 17th century and was rebuilt.

The small gatehouse, dating from the 16th century, defends the entrance to the palace and has gun ports, as well as the painted panels for the orders of knighthood bestowed on James V: The Golden Fleece, St Michael, The Garter, and The Thistle.

There was a 12th-century castle here, which was captured and strengthened by Edward I of England in 1301 during the Wars of Independence. It was slighted, after being retaken by the Scots by driving a cart under the portcullis,

Linlithgow Palace

Linlithgow Palace, Great Hall fireplace

and remained a ruin until about 1350. It was repaired by David II, then mostly rebuilt by James I at the beginning of the 15th century. It became a favourite residence of the kings of Scots, and the work continued under James III and James IV. Mary, Queen of Scots, was born here in 1542.

After the Union of the Crowns in 1603, the palace was left in the charge of a keeper and the north range collapsed and was rebuilt for James VI. It was last used by Charles I in 1633 although his son, James, Duke of York, stayed here before succeeding to the throne as James VII in 1685. In the 1650s, Cromwell had garrisoned the palace. It was also visited by Queen Anne with her father in the 1680s, Bonnie Prince Charlie in 1745, and the Duke of Cumberland the next year. General Hawley retreated here after being defeated by the Jacobites at the nearby Battle of Falkirk. The soldiers started fires to dry themselves, and the palace was accidentally set ablaze. It was never restored.

The palace is said to be haunted by a Blue Lady, who walks from the entrance of the palace to near the door of the nearby parish church of St Michael. Queen Margaret's bower, at the top of one of the stair-towers, is reputed to be haunted by the ghost of either Margaret Tudor, wife of James IV, or Mary of Guise, wife of James V, although – it has to be said – neither candidate seems very likely. The apparition is described as a White Lady in one account, and said to be accompanied by a smell of perfume. An apparition of Mary, Queen of Scots, is also reputed to have been seen praying in the chapel.

It was in the adjacent parish church of St Michael that a blue-robed apparition is said to have warned James IV not to march into England – but the king ignored the warning, invaded England, and was killed at the disastrous Battle of Flodden in 1513. The church is a fine building with a unique crown design atop the steeple and is open to the public.

Linlithgow Palace, courtyard and fountain

The palace is in a scenic spot in a park and there are walks around the loch, while Linlithgow is a pleasant town with places to eat and shop, a heritage trail and the Annet House Museum and terraced garden on the High Street.

18 miles west of Edinburgh, 33 miles east and north of Glasgow, in Linlithgow, off A803, at Linlithgow Palace (signposted).
NT 003774   OS: 65   EH49 7AL
Historic Scotland: open Apr-Sep, daily 9.30-17.30; Oct-Mar, daily 9.30-16.30; last ticket sold 45 mins before closing; closed 25/26 Dec and 1/2 Jan.
Tel: 01506 842896   Web: www.historic-scotland.gov.uk
Features: Parking. Shop. Refreshments (cafe nearby). WC. Partial disabled access. Admission charged.
St Michael's Parish Church open May-Sep, daily; Oct-Mar, Mon-Fri.
Tel: 01506 842188   Web: www.stmichaels-parish.org.uk
Annet House Museum open Apr-Sep, Mon-Sat 11.00-17.00, Sun 13.00-16.00
Tel: 01506 670677   Web: www.annethousemuseum.org.uk
Nearest:
The Binns (4 miles)
Blackness Castle (4 miles)
Callendar House (8 miles)
Hopetoun House (11 miles)
Lauriston Castle (15 miles)

Lochleven Castle

Colour photo page C47

On a sylvan island in the loch (a National Nature Reserve), Lochleven Castle consists of a small 15th-century tower, rectangular in plan, of five storeys, standing at one corner of a 14th-century courtyard. A corbelled-out parapet, with three open rounds, crowns the tower. The courtyard has a small round tower, with gunloops, at one corner, and the entrance is through an arched gateway. The courtyard enclosed ranges of buildings, including a hall and kitchen, but these are very ruinous. The castle used to occupy most of the island, but the level of the loch has been lowered.

The original entrance to the main tower was at second-floor level, from an external stair, and leads to the hall through a hooded arch. A turnpike stair leads down to the vaulted kitchen on the first floor. The basement is also vaulted, but has a modern entrance. The chamber above the hall has an oratory, with altar-shelf and piscina.

Lochleven was a royal castle from 1257, and was stormed by William Wallace after being captured by the English. The English besieged the castle in 1301, but it was relieved by Sir John Comyn before it could be captured. It was visited by Robert the Bruce in 1313 and 1323. The castle was held again against Edward Balliol and the English in 1335. By the end of the 14th century, it had passed to the Douglases of Lochleven. Mary, Queen of Scots, was held

Lochleven Castle

Lochleven Castle, main tower

in the main tower from 1567 until she escaped in 1568, during which time she signed her abdication and is believed to have had a miscarriage, perhaps of twins – her ghost is said to haunt the castle.

The property passed to the Bruces of Kinross. Kinross House, a large classical mansion and one of the finest examples of 17th-century architecture in Scotland, was built by Sir William Bruce, Royal Architect to Charles II. There are formal walled gardens and Lochleven Castle was part of the designed landscape.

28 miles north of Edinburgh, 32 miles south-west of Dundee, 1 mile east of Kinross, off B996, on Castle Island in Loch Leven, Lochleven Castle (signposted).
NO 138018   OS: 58   KY13 8UF
Historic Scotland: open Apr-Sep, daily 9.30-17.30; Oct, daily 9.30-16.30; last ticket sold 60 mins before closing – includes ferry trip from Kinross.
Tel: 01577 862670   Web: www.historic-scotland.gov.uk
Features: Parking (Kinross, near ferry). Shop. Refreshments nearby. WC. Picnic area. No disabled access. Admission charged.
Castle Campbell (13 miles)
Falkland Palace (13 miles)
Aberdour Castle (14 miles)
Elcho Castle (19 miles)
Hopetoun House (20 miles)

MANDERSTON

Colour photos page C49

Nestling in attractive grounds and policies, Manderston is a fine and substantial Edwardian mansion of three storeys and an attic, part of which dates from the original house of 1790 (perhaps with even earlier work). The building has fine Adam-style interiors and features the only silver staircase in the world.

Manderston was held by the Manderston family in the 15th century and there was a strong castle here, but had passed to the Homes of Manderston by 1568. Sir George Home of Manderston was involved in witchcraft accusations, which even involved Helen Arnot, his wife. She was not on good terms with her husband and may have had cause to revert to witchcraft to rid herself of him. The lady was cleared, but many others were executed in Edinburgh in 1630. The lands had gone to the Swintons by the middle of the 18th century, and then by the end of that century to the Weatherstones.

The house was completely remodelled between 1903-5 by the architect John Kinross for Sir James Miller, a millionaire racehorse owner, who made a fortune trading hemp and herrings with the Russians. His brother had acquired the property in 1855, and it later passed by marriage to the Palmer Lords Palmer. Among many other attractions, Manderston is home to the extensive Huntly and Palmer Biscuit Tin Museum.

The house stands in 56 acres of formal and informal gardens with a pond, and there is a fine marble dairy in a mock tower house and cloister.

The Channel 4 series *The Edwardian House* was filmed at Manderston.

Manderston

Manderston, Marble Dairy and Tower House

44 miles east and south of Edinburgh, 14 miles west of Berwick-upon-Tweed, 1.5 miles east of Duns, on A6105, at Manderston (signposted). NT 810545 OS: 74 TD11 3PP

Open early May-late Sep, Thu and Sun 13.30-17.00, last entry 45 mins before closing; Bank Holiday open Mon May and Aug, 13.30-17.00; other times group (min 15) visits by appt; gardens and tearoom open 11.30. Venue for events, dinners, parties or weddings.

Tel: 01361 882636 Web: www.manderston.co.uk

Features: Parking. Gift shop. Tea room. WC. Gardens. Admission charged.

Nearest:

Paxton House (10 miles)
Gunsgreen House (12 miles)
Mellerstain (16 miles)
Floors Castle (21 miles)
Thirlestane Castle (21 miles)

MELLERSTAIN

Colour photos pages C50 & C51

Arguably the best Adam house in Scotland, Mellerstain is a magnificent castellated mansion in beautifully landscaped grounds. It was designed by the architects William Adam and his famous son, Robert. The wings date from 1725 and were designed by William, while the central block by Robert was not completed until 1778. There are fabulous, largely unaltered interiors, especially the library, music room (former dining room) and drawing room, with carefully designed proportions, classical plasterwork and friezes, and glowing colours. The great gallery is another outstanding chamber. The house has a large collection of art, as well as a colourful terraced garden, and stands in 200 acres of scenic parkland with a lake, a canal and extensive woodland.

The lands of Mellerstain were mentioned in 1451, when they were given to the Halyburton family but by 1642 had passed to the Baillies of Jerviswood, Jerviswood being a property near Lanark. The family were Covenanters and Robert Baillie was arrested for treason and sentenced to death. The Baillies were then ruined after being heavily fined and forfeited, although their fortune was restored in 1691 after the overthrow of James VII.

Mellerstain was built for George Baillie of Jerviswood, replacing an old tower house, and was home to Lady Grisell Home, better known now as Grisell

Mellerstain

Mellerstain

Baillie. Grisell who when young had been involved in the intrigues of the Covenanting times, was a poet also compiled her famous *Household Accounts,* an insight into the everyday workings of a stately home, in the 18th century.

Mellerstain passed by marriage to Charles Hamilton, Lord Binning, eldest son of the Earl of Haddington, and was held by the Baillie-Hamiltons, Earls of Haddington, until 1987. It is now owned by The Mellerstain Trust.

40 miles south-east of Edinburgh, 8 miles north-west of Kelso, west of A6089 or east of B6397, at Mellerstain (signposted).
NT 648392   OS: 74   TD3 6LG
Open Easter wknd (Fri-Mon), then May-Sep, Fri-Mon 12.30-17.00, last entry 16.15; gardens and coffee shop same days, 11.30-17.00; groups by appt all year; holiday cottages on estate; weddings and events.
Tel: 01573 410225   Web: www.mellerstain.com
Features: Parking. Gift shop. Coffee shop (opens 11.30). WC. Disabled access to main floor, lower floor and garden terrace. Gardens and parkland. Admission charged.
Floors Castle (7 miles)
Thirlestane Castle (12 miles)
Abbotsford (13 miles)
Manderston (17 miles)
Bowhill House (20 miles)

MOUNT STUART

Colour photos pages C52 & C53

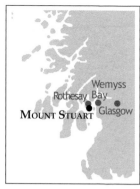

Scotland's finest Victorian Gothic stately home with splendid interior decoration, Mount Stuart was designed by the architect Robert Rowand Anderson for John, 3rd Marquess of Bute. John was one of the wealthiest men of his day, and had wide interests in history, astrology, archaeology, as well as being an industrial magnate and philanthropist – and Keeper of Rothesay Castle. The present Mount Stuart was built on the site of an earlier house of 1719, designed by Alexander McGill, which was burnt down in a disastrous fire of 1877, although one wing survives. The house is still the seat of the Crichton-Stuart Marquesses of Bute, who also formerly owned Dumfries House.

The house has a sumptuous interior throughout, not least the stunning Marble Hall, 80 foot high with tiers of gothic arches and richly coloured stained glass, symbolising the signs of the zodiac, and the chapel in dazzling white marble.

The house is surrounded by 300 acres of fine landscaped grounds, gardens and woodlands with an adventure play area and an octagonal glass pavilion with tropical plants. Rothesay Castle is also open the public.

Mount Stuart

156

Mount Stuart, Chapel

89 miles west of Edinburgh, 46 miles west of Glasgow, 5 miles south of Rothesay, off A844, Mount Stuart (signposted), Island of Bute (CalMac ferries from Wemyss Bay on mainland to Rothesay or Colintraive on Cowal to north of Bute).
NS 105595   OS: 63   PA20 9LR
House and garden open for guided tours Easter-Sep, daily 11.00-16.00, last house entry 15.00; gardens 10.00-18.00; wedding and events venue.
Tel: 01700 503877   Web: www.mountstuart.com
Features: Parking. Gift shop. Restaurant. WC. Picnic areas. Landscaped grounds, gardens and woodland. Glass pavilion. Adventure play area. Disabled facilities: access to house and most of gardens. Buses stop at entrance to visitor centre. Admission charged. Inclusive travel tickets available from CalMac at Wemyss Bay (ferry / bus / entrance / guided tour).
Rothesay Castle (5 miles)
Newark Castle (24 miles (ferry))
Pollok House (45 miles (ferry))
Brodick Castle, Arran (47 miles (two ferries))
Inveraray Castle (56 miles (ferry))

NEWARK CASTLE

Colour photo page C54

Standing on the shore of the Clyde, Newark Castle is a solid and impressive building. The castle consists of a simple square 15th-century tower, to which was added a 16th-century gatehouse range and then a large late 16th-century block, to form three sides of a courtyard. The remaining side was formerly completed by a wall.

The old tower rises to four storeys, the top storey being built from the original parapet. The tall gatehouse block is three storeys high with a gabled roof. An arched gateway leads to a vaulted pend, which opens into the courtyard.

The later large range has bartizans at the corners, and the walls are pierced by gunloops. A semi-circular stair-tower, with a conical roof, is corbelled out above first-floor level. This building is dated 1597.

The basement is vaulted and contains a kitchen, with a wide fireplace, a cellar, and a wine-cellar with a small stair to the hall above. The hall, on the first floor and reached by the main stair, has a richly decorated fireplace. The second storey contains a gallery. One chamber has original panelling with bed press and door, and a painted ceiling.

Newark was originally a property of the Dennistouns or Danielstouns, but passed by marriage to the Maxwells of Calderwood in 1402, who built the castle. James IV was a frequent visitor when prosecuting his campaign against the Lords of the Isles. One of the family, Patrick Maxwell, was involved in the murders of Patrick Maxwell of Stanely and the Montgomery Earl of Eglinton,

Newark Castle

158

Newark Castle, Hall

in 1584 and 1596 respectively, during a series of feuds. He was married to Margaret Crawford for some 44 years and had 16 children, although he beat and so mistreated Margaret that she left him. She died in poverty.

In 1668 another Patrick Maxwell sold the land to the city of Glasgow so that a new port could be built, the name being changed from Newark to Port Glasgow. The castle was latterly occupied by poorer folk, but was handed over into State care in 1909 and partly restored.

There are stories that the castle is haunted, reputedly by a blonde-haired woman seen in red, and reported to be witnessed in the steward's chamber of the gatehouse. This has been identified by some as the bogle of Margaret Crawford, who is mentioned above.

68 miles west of Edinburgh, 21 miles west of Glasgow, just to east of Port Glasgow, off A8, on the south shore of the Clyde, at Newark Castle (signposted).
NS 328745   OS: 63   PA14 5NH
Historic Scotland: open Apr-Sep, daily 9.30-17.30; last entry 30 mins before closing. Venue for weddings and events.
Tel: 01475 741858   Web: www.historic-scotland.gov.uk
Features: Parking. Shop. Refreshments. WC. Disabled access to ground floor. Park. Admission charged.
Rothesay Castle, Bute (19 miles (ferry))
Pollok House (20 miles)
Mount Stuart, Bute (24 miles (ferry))
Bothwell Castle (29 miles)
Dean Castle (34 miles)

NEWHAILES

Colour photo page C54

In landscaped parkland and woodland overlooking the Forth, Newhailes is a plain and somewhat dour although imposing symmetrical mansion. The first more modest house was built in 1686 by the architect James Smith as his own residence, but this was altered and extended in the 18th century with the addition of new wings including a splendid library. There are fine rococo interiors, decorated with many shells, including the library, and there is a good collection of paintings and portraits.

The property was formerly known as Whitehill, and was held by the Preston family from the 15th century. James Smith purchased Whitehill in 1686, was Surveyor of the Royal Works, and began the present Newhailes. Smith got into financial difficulties and sold the property to John Bellenden of Broughton, 2nd Lord Bellenden, in 1702, who renamed it Broughton. The name was changed to Newhailes when the property was purchased in 1709 by Sir David Dalrymple, calling it after his East Lothian estate of Hailes, and he extended the house.

Newhailes was visited by many leading figures of the Scottish

Newhailes

Newhailes, Dining Room

Enlightenment. The house was occupied as a private residence until 1997 and much of the atmospheric and homely interior has been preserved as it was left.

6 miles east of Edinburgh, 1.5 miles west and south of Musselburgh, off A6095 (Newhailes Road), at Newhailes (signposted).
NT 325725   OS: 66   EH21 6RY
NTS: House open for guided tours: open Easter, then May-Sep, Thu-Mon 12.00-15.30 (last tour); visitor centre with cafe open same days as house, plus Oct, Sat & Sun; estate open all year, daily until dusk.
Tel: 0844 493 2125   Web: www.nts.org.uk
Features: Parking (charge). Shop. Cafe. WC. Plant centre. Grounds. Limited disabled access to house. Admission charged. Beware of dogs in the grounds…
Nearest:
Craigmillar Castle (3 miles)
Palace of Holyroodhouse (5 miles)
Edinburgh Castle (6 miles)
Lauriston Castle (10 miles)
Crichton Castle (11 miles)

PALACE OF HOLYROODHOUSE

Colour photo page C55

HOLYROODHOUSE
Glasgow   Edinburgh

A fine and impressive edifice at the foot of the Royal Mile, Holyroodhouse consists of ranges surrounding a rectangular courtyard, one of which dates from the 16th century with towers capped by conical roofs. The walls of the old part are pierced by gunloops. The present building was designed by Sir William Bruce for Charles II in 1671-8. It stands by the ruinous church of Holyrood Abbey and near the new Scottish Parliament building.

Holyrood Abbey was founded by David I around 1128 although it was sacked in 1322 and 1385 by the English. James III found the guest range of the abbey a comfortable alternative to Edinburgh Castle, and James IV and James V extended the building. The English burnt the abbey in 1544 and 1547, and all that survived their destruction was a block, with round corner towers (as mentioned above), built in 1529 to contain private chambers for James V.

David Rizzio, Mary, Queen of Scots's secretary, was murdered here in her presence by men led by her husband, Lord Darnley, in 1566. A plaque marks the spot (reputedly along with a blood stain which cannot be washed off), and he is buried in the nearby Canongate Cemetery. The palace was rebuilt in the

Palace of Holyroodhouse

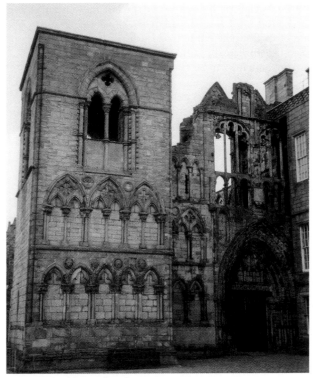

Holyrood Abbey, church

late 17th century, a new block being built to balance the original tower with a connecting wall. The original 16th-century interiors survive in the old block.

Bonnie Prince Charlie stayed here for six weeks in 1745, and held court after the Battle of Prestonpans, while the Duke of Cumberland made it his residence after the Rising. The palace is the official residence of the monarch in Scotland.

The State Apartments have fine plasterwork and house Brussels tapestries and paintings, while the Great Gallery has portraits of over 80 kings of Scots, painted by Jacob de Wet in 1684-6, (and nearly all entirely made up from his imagination). There is also access to the apartments where Mary, Queen of Scots, stayed, including Mary's Bedchamber and the Outer Chamber, where Rizzio was murdered in 1566.

A Grey Lady, thought to be the spirit of one of Mary's companions, has reputedly been seen in the Queen's Audience Chamber. Ghostly footsteps are said to have been heard in the long gallery.

The fine ruins of the abbey church adjoin the palace, and can also be visited. The east end of the building was demolished, while the surviving part was made the Chapel Royal. It was ransacked in 1688 and the roof collapsed 80 years later. The church is the burial place of David II, James V and Henry Stewart, Lord Darnley, although the kings' tombs were despoiled by the English in attacks of 1544 and 1547.

The Queen's Gallery, housed in the shell of the former Holyrood Free Church and refurbished and opened in 2002, has a programme of changing exhibitions of art from the Royal Collection.

The Scottish Parliament stands at the foot of the Royal Mile, near the Palace, and the building can be visited.

> 47 miles west of Glasgow, 1 mile east of Edinburgh Castle, off A1, on the north-east edge of Holyrood Park, opposite the Scottish Parliament Building, at the foot of the Royal Mile (Canongate), at Palace of Holyroodhouse (signposted).
> NT 269739   OS: 66   EH8 8DX
> Open all year (except during royal visits): Apr-Oct, daily 9.30-18.00, last admission 16.30; Nov-Mar, daily 9.30-16.30, last admission 15.15; closed 25-26 Dec.
> Tel: 0131 556 5100   Web: www.royalcollection.org.uk
> Features: Parking nearby. Gift shop. Cafe. WC. Queen's Gallery (combined admission with Palace). Disabled access, although not to Mary Queen of Scot's chambers. Admission charged.
> Queen's Gallery open Apr-Oct, daily 9.30-18.00, last entry 17.00; Nov-Mar, 9.30-16.30, last admission 15.30; closed some days in Nov and 25-26 Dec.
> Nearest:
> Edinburgh Castle (1 mile)
> Craigmillar Castle (4 miles)
> Lauriston Castle (5 miles)
> Newhailes (5 miles)
> Crichton Castle (14 miles)

Scottish Parliament and Palace of Holyroodhouse, Edinburgh

PAXTON HOUSE

Colour photos page C56

In picturesque gardens and wooded grounds overlooking the Tweed (the English Border), Paxton House is an elegant and largely unaltered classical mansion. The house has a central block, with a portico and columns, and two flanking wings, one of which housed the original kitchen, the other the stables.

The house was built in 1758 to the designs of the architect John Adam for Patrick Home of Billie. The house was for his intended bride, Sophie de Brandt, from the court of King Frederick the Great of Prussia, but their respective parents managed to put an end to their romance and the marriage never happened; within a few years Sophie was dead.

The twelve period rooms hold an extensive collection of Chippendale and Trotter furniture, with both fine rococo and Adam interiors, including magnificent ceilings and plaster work. The sinuous main stair has an unusual wrought iron bannister. The Regency Picture Gallery was added in 1811 to the designs of Robert Reid, and is the largest in a Scottish country house, housing more than 70 paintings from the National Galleries of Scotland.

The lands were held by the Paxton family in the 14th century, and Adam of Paxton was outlawed for holding Dunbar Castle against James III in 1479. The property passed to the Homes of Wedderburn. Sir George Home, 3rd Baronet of Wedderburn, was a Jacobite. He was captured at the Battle of Preston in 1716 and was sentenced to death, and although he was later reprieved, the

Paxton House

165

Paxton House, Old Kitchen

property was forfeited. Wedderburn was bought back by his kinsmen, Rev Ninian Home of Billie. His son Patrick built the house.

At Paxton are 80 acres of garden, woodland with a walk along the banks of the River Tweed, and park land, as well as red-squirrel and wild-bird viewing hides. Paxton House is in the care of the Paxton Trust.

60 miles east and south of Edinburgh, 4 miles west and south of Berwick-upon-Tweed, south of B6461, at Paxton House (signposted). NT 935530 OS: 74 TD15 1SZ

Open Apr-early Nov, daily for guided tours 11.00-17.00, last tour 15.30; other times for groups by appt; shop and tearoom, 10.00-17.00; tearoom also open in winter, Nov-mid Dec, then early Feb-Mar, Wed-Sun 11.00-15.00 (check with house); grounds 10.00-sunset. Venue for weddings and events. Holiday apartment available.

Tel: 01289 386291 Web: www.paxtonhouse.com

Facilities: Parking. Gift shop. Tea room. WC. Limited disabled access. Art exhibitions. Gardens, grounds and woodland walk. Caravan park. Admission charged.

Nearest:
Gunsgreen House (10 miles)
Manderston (10 miles)
Floors Castle (20 miles)
Mellerstain (22 miles)
Thirlestane Castle (28 miles)

POLLOK HOUSE

Colour photo page C55

Pollok House is a grand and impressive classical mansion, first built about 1750, and then remodelled and extended by the architect Sir Robert Rowand Anderson in 1890. There is a lavish interior and the Stirling Maxwell collection of Spanish and European paintings, including works by El Greco, Goya and Murillo, furniture, ceramics and silver. There is also a hand-made model of Crookston Castle, carved from a branch of The Crookston Yew under which Mary, Queen of Scots, is said to have pledged her troth to Henry Stewart, Lord Darnley. Pollok House replaced an old castle, a vestige of which remains in a garden wall, which itself had replaced older strongholds.

The house stands among colourful gardens, parkland and woodland.

Pollok was a property of the Pollok family, but passed by marriage to the Maxwells in the mid 13th century and they held estate for some 600 years. The Maxwells abandoned Pollok in favour of their new castle at Haggs in 1585, but returned in 1753 when the present Pollok House was completed.

In 1676 Sir George Maxwell of Pollok took part in a witch trial in Gourock. Shortly afterwards he believed himself bewitched, suffering a 'hot and fiery distemper'. Janet Douglas, who could not speak, disclosed that his effigies were to be found stuck with pins at the house of Janet Mathie, widow to the miller of Shaw Mill. Janet, her son John Stewart, her daughter Annabel, and another

Pollok House

167

Pollok House

three women were tried in Paisley in 1677. Annabel was only 14 years old and was released, the others were throttled and burned at the stake. Sir George recovered, but lived for only a few months, although Janet recovered her speech. The story has been dramatised for the stage.

Pollok was used as a military hospital during World War I, and was gifted to the City of Glasgow in 1966 while the policies are now a country park. The Burrell Collection is situated within the grounds, but displays only a fraction of Sir William Burrell's collection of artwork, armour, weaponry and other antiquities, so the collection is frequently changed.

51 miles west of Edinburgh, 6 miles south-west of Glasgow Cathedral, in Pollokshaws, west of B768 or B769, north of Haggs Road and west of Dumbreck Road, 0.75 miles south of M77 at Dumbreck Interchange, Pollok Country Park, at Pollok House (signposted).
NS 549619   OS: 64   G43 1AT
NTS: open all year, daily 10.00-17.00, last entry 16.30; closed 25-26 Dec and 1-2 Jan. Venue for weddings and events.
Tel: 0844 493 2202   Web: www.nts.org.uk
Features: Parking. Gift shop. Licensed restaurant. WC. Partial disabled access. Murder mystery evenings (Aug). Gardens and park. Admission charged.
Bothwell Castle (12 miles)
Dean Castle (19 miles)
Newark Castle (20 miles)
Craignethan Castle (26 miles)
Stirling Castle (33 miles)

ROTHESAY CASTLE

Colour photo page C57

Surrounded by a wet moat and built on a round mound, Rothesay Castle has an enormous 12th-century circular shell keep, with four later massive round towers. In the late 15th century a large rectangular tower and gatehouse were added, built for comfort as well as defence, and then completed by James V after 1541. Parts of the castle were restored in the late 19th century. The sea was formerly much closer to the castle.

The entrance leads through a long vaulted passage, in the floor of which is a trapdoor to a pit-prison. The first-floor hall can be reached by a narrow mural stair or by external steps within the castle walls. There were private chambers on the floors above the hall.

The castle was attacked by Norsemen in the 1230s, who cut a hole in the wall with their axes. It was taken in 1263 by King Haakon of Norway, before he was defeated at the Battle of Largs. The Stewarts were keepers of the castle. Rothesay was held by the English during the Wars of Independence, but was taken by Robert the Bruce, only to be captured again by the English in 1334, to be recaptured once again by the Scots.

This was a favoured residence of Robert II and Robert III, who died here in 1406. In 1401 Robert III made his son, David, Duke of Rothesay, a title since taken by the eldest son of the kings of Scots and currently held by Prince Charles (David, himself, did not fare so well and was starved to death at Falkland

Rothesay Castle, curtain wall and tower

Rothesay Castle, courtyard

before he could be king). The castle was besieged by the Lord of the Isles in 1462, the Master of Ruthven in 1527, and in 1544 was captured by the Earl of Lennox on behalf of the English. It had been visited by James V, who completed the gatehouse block. In the 1650s it was held for Charles I, but later taken by Cromwell, whose men damaged the castle.

Argyll's forces torched the castle in 1685, and it was very ruinous until repaired and partly rebuilt by the Marquess of Bute. The Crichton-Stuart Marquesses of Bute live at Mount Stuart, further south on the island.

Rothesay has many places to eat, and among its attractions are the Bute Museum on Stuart Street, near the castle, and the impressive men's Victorian toilets at the Pier. There are also facilities for women, just not so plush.

87 miles east of Edinburgh, 39 miles west of Glasgow, in Rothesay on island of Bute, off A886, at Rothesay Castle (signposted). CalMac run ferries from Wemyss Bay on mainland to Rothesay on Bute or Colintraive on Cowal to north of Bute.
NS 086646 OS: 63
Historic Scotland: open Apr-Sep, daily 9.30-17.30; Oct-Mar, Sat-Wed 9.30-16.30, closed Thu & Fri; last ticket sold 30 mins before closing; closed 25/26 Dec and 1/2 Jan.
Tel: 01700 502691 Web: www.historic-scotland.gov.uk
Features: Parking nearby. Kiosk. WC. Admission charged.
Mount Stuart (5 miles)
Newark Castle (19 miles (ferry))
Pollok House (39 miles (ferry))
Brodick Castle, Arran (42 miles (two ferries))
Inveraray Castle (51 miles (ferry))

SCONE PALACE

Colour photo page C57

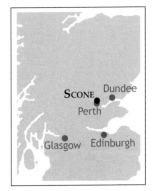

In 100 acres of policies, wild gardens, woodlands and a pinetum, Scone Palace is a large and imposing gothic mansion, dating from 1802 and designed by the architect William Atkinson. The name is pronounced 'Skoon', and the palace incorporates part of the house built by the Ruthvens in the 1580s, itself probably created out of the Abbot's Lodging of the former abbey. The fine grounds are also home to peacocks, including white males.

The palace has a sumptuous interior, and a particularly grand feature is the royal gallery, which is some 142 foot long

Scone was a centre of the Picts, and in the 6th century a Culdee cell of the early Celtic church was founded here. The Kings of Scots were inaugurated at the Moot Hill, near the present palace, from the reign of Kenneth MacAlpin, including MacBeth, Malcolm Canmore, Robert the Bruce and the first four Jameses. An abbey had been founded here in the 12th century, and the Stone of Destiny, also called the Stone of Scone, on which the monarchs were crowned, was kept here, until taken to Westminster Abbey by Edward I of England in 1296 – although this was returned to Edinburgh Castle in 1996. The last king to be inaugurated at Scone was Charles II in 1651, who also stayed at the palace.

The abbey was sacked by a Protestant mob in 1559 and there are no obvious remains, while the lands went to the Ruthvens in 1580. However, after the Gowrie Conspiracy in 1600, when John Ruthven, 3rd Earl of Gowrie, and his

Scone Palace

171

Scone Palace

brother, Alexander, the Master of Ruthven, were slain by James VI and others, Scone passed to the Murrays. Sir David Murray of Gospertie had been one of those to save the king's life – or at least to stop James being forcibly kidnapped. The Murrays moved from Balvaird Castle, and were made Viscounts Stormont in 1602, and then Earls of Mansfield in 1776.

James VIII and III held 'court' at Scone in 1716 during the Jacobite Risings, and Bonnie Prince Charlie visited in 1745.

The old village of Scone was moved to New Scone in 1804-5, as it was too close to the Palace for the then owners. On the Moot Hill is Scone Palace Chapel, used as a mausoleum and containing the exuberant alabaster monument to commemorate David Murray, 1st Viscount Stormont. The palace is still home to the Murray Earls of Mansfield, Viscounts Stormont and Lords Scone and Lords Balvaird, who are also hereditary Keepers of Lochmaben Castle.

45 miles north of Edinburgh, 2.5 miles north of Perth, on A93, east of River Tay, at Scone Palace (signposted).
NO 114267   OS: 58   PH2 6BD
Open Apr-Oct, daily 9.30-last admission at 17.00; grounds close at 17.45; other times by appt; grounds, coffee shop and food shop, open Nov-Mar, Fri-Sun, 10.00-16.00. Venue for weddings, meetings and events. Sporting estate.
Tel: 01738 552300   Web: www.scone-palace.co.uk
Features: Parking. Gift and food shop. Restaurant. Tearoom. WC. Picnic area. 100 acres of wild gardens. Maze. Adventure playground. Disabled access to state rooms & restaurant. Admission charged.
Huntingtower (5 miles)
Elcho Castle (8 miles)
Lochleven Castle (21 miles)
Drummond Castle Gardens (24 miles)
Glamis Castle (27 miles)

SKIPNESS CASTLE

Colour photo page C58

With fine views over the Kilbrannan Sound to Arran, Skipness Castle is a 13th-century castle of enclosure, later consisting of a courtyard with a curtain wall, a tower house and ranges of buildings. The wall has three ruined towers. The main entrance was from the sea, which was defended by a gatetower, with a portcullis and a machiolation.

The 16th-century tower house rises to four storeys and a garret, and incorporates a late 13th-century tower or earlier hall-house. The parapet has open rounds at three corners, and a gabled caphouse at the other. The basement is vaulted, and has no access to the floors above. The hall is reached by an external stone stair, while a mural stair climbs to the second floor.

The first castle was probably built by the MacSweens around 1247, and it was strengthened against the Vikings about 1262. It was held by the MacDonald Lords of the Isles until 1493, when they were forfeited. The castle was then granted to the Forresters, but in 1499 it was acquired by the Campbell Earl of Argyll. It was besieged unsuccessfully by Alaisdair Colkitto MacDonald in the 1640s, but was abandoned at the end of the 17th century, then being used as a farm steading with the demolishing of the early courtyard buildings.

Near the castle is Skipness House, built for the Graham family at the end of the 19th century, although it incorporates some of a much older house.

Skipness Castle

173

Skipness Castle

The ruins of a 13th-century chapel, Kilbrannan, dedicated to St Brendan, lie to the south-east of the castle. There are fine graveslabs and excellent views across to Arran, and members of the Campbells are buried here.

Skipness is said to have a *gruagach*, a Green Lady, described as being as small as a child but dressed in green and with golden hair. The spirit would clean and tidy, and feed hens; but it is also accused of nearly killing a man it believed was sleeping in the wrong bed. She was also reported to have the ability to confuse enemies attacking the castle, so thwarting attempts to seize Skipness.

113 miles west of Glasgow, 160 miles east of Edinburgh, 62 miles south of Oban, 12 miles south of Tarbert, off end of B8001 at Skipness, at Skipness Castle (signposted)
NR 907577   OS: 62   PA29 6XU
Historic Scotland: access at all reasonable times; short walk to castle, then longer walk to chapel, which may be muddy. The tower is open Apr-Sep, but closed Oct-Mar.
Web: www.historic-scotland.gov.uk
Features: Parking near castle.
Nearest:
Brodick Castle, Arran (20 miles (ferry))
Carnasserie Castle (35 miles)
Inveraray Castle (50 miles)
Kilchurn Castle (65 miles)
Dunstaffnage Castle (66 miles)

SPYNIE PALACE

Colour photo page C58

One of the finest fortresses in Scotland, Spynie Palace consists of a massive 15th-century tower (the largest in Scotland, by volume!) at one corner of a large courtyard, enclosed by a wall, with square corner towers. In one wall is a gatehouse, and there were ranges of buildings, including a chapel, within the courtyard walls. The main tower, David's Tower, rises six storeys to the parapet, and has very thick walls. The corbels for the parapet survive, and the walls are pierced by gunloops. There are fine views from the top of the tower.

There were two entrances at basement level, one from the courtyard into the basement, and one, a postern, from outside the walls, which opens onto a stair to the first floor. The courtyard entrance led to the vaulted basement.

The main entrance, on the first floor, is approached by a stair up a mound. It leads, through a lobby, to a turnpike stair in one corner, and to a guardroom in the thickness of the wall. The hall, on the first floor, was a fine chamber with a large moulded fireplace and windows with stone seats. Five vaulted chambers, one above another, are built into the thickness of one wall, although these have been rebuilt. The top floor was vaulted, but this has collapsed, and has been replaced by a modern roof of a 'unique' design.

Spynie Palace

175

One corner tower of five storeys survives, as does a section of curtain wall and the gatehouse, but the rest of the courtyard is ruined. The elaborate gatehouse was defended by a portcullis.

In 1200 Bishop Richard moved the cathedral of Moray to Spynie, where it stayed for 24 years. Later bishops fortified a promontory in Spynie Loch, once a sea loch with its own port, and although the cathedral was moved to Elgin, they kept their residence and stronghold here. Over the next two centuries they built the grandest surviving bishop's palace in Scotland.

The palace was probably built by Bishop Innes, just after Elgin Cathedral had been burnt by Alexander Stewart, the Wolf of Badenoch. Bishop David Stewart, who died in 1475, excommunicated the Gordon Earl of Huntly, and built the great tower, David's Tower, to defend himself against retribution by Huntly. James IV visited the palace in 1493 and 1505, as did Mary, Queen of Scots in 1562. James Hepburn, Earl of Bothwell and third husband of Mary, sheltered here after defeat at the Battle of Carberry Hill in 1567, but soon fled north to Orkney and the Continent.

After the Reformation, the lands were sold to the Lindsays, but the castle was subsequently used by Protestant bishops. James VI stayed here in 1589. General Munro besieged the castle in 1640, and compelled Bishop Guthrie to surrender it, and he was imprisoned. The castle was held by Innes of Innes and Grant of Ballindalloch – who were Covenanters – against the Gordon Earl of Huntly, who besieged the palace unsuccessfully in 1645, while acting for the Marquis of Montrose. The last resident bishop was Colin Falconer, who died here in 1686, and Bishop Hay, the last incumbent, was removed from office in 1688. The building then became ruinous, and was stripped.

There were stories of the bishops being in league with the Devil, and that every Halloween witches would be seen flying to the castle. The castle is also reputedly haunted, and unexplained lights and unearthly music are said to have been witnessed here. There also stories of a phantom piper and a ghostly lion.

By Cooper Park with a Biblical Garden, boating pond and much else, Elgin Cathedral is a substantial and picturesque ruin in the pretty former city of Elgin. The Elgin Museum is on the High Street.

176 miles north of Edinburgh, 40 miles west of Inverness, 70 miles north-west of Aberdeen, 2.5 miles north of Elgin, off A941, at Spynie Palace (signposted).
NJ 231658   OS: 28   IV30 5QG
Historic Scotland: open Apr-Sep, daily 9.30-17.30.
Tel: 01343 546358   Web: www.historic-scotland.gov.uk
Features: Parking. Gift shop. WC. Picnic area. Limited disabled access. Admission charged. Joint ticket with Elgin Cathedral available (cathedral open Apr-Sep, daily; Oct-Mar, Sat-Wed).
Nearest:
Brodie Castle (18 miles)
Balvenie Castle (20 miles)
Ballindalloch Castle (25 miles)
Cawdor Castle (28 miles)
Huntly Castle (30 miles)

ST ANDREWS CASTLE

Colour photo page C59

Close to the remains of the cathedral, St Andrews Castle is a ruined courtyard castle, enclosed by a wall. There was a gatehouse and towers at the corners, one of which contained a bottle dungeon dug out of the rock. Much of the castle is very ruined.

The first castle here was built by Bishop Roger, but was dismantled by Robert the Bruce around 1310. It was rebuilt in 1336 by the English, but was captured by Sir Andrew Moray in 1337, and slighted again. At the end of the 14th century, Bishop Walter Trail rebuilt the castle. Patrick Graham, the first archbishop, was deposed and imprisoned here in 1478. Archbishop Alexander Stewart, natural son of James IV, was killed at the Battle of Flodden in 1513.

Cardinal David Beaton, who was also archbishop, strengthened the castle. After George Wishart had been burned alive for heresy, a party of Protestants broke into the castle and murdered Beaton in 1546, and hung his naked body from one of the towers. His corpse went unburied for some seven months, having been left in a barrel of salt water in the bottle dungeon. Reinforced by others, including John Knox, the Protestants held the castle for a year. The besiegers tunnelled towards the walls, and the defenders countermined and captured their tunnel. Both tunnels still survive and can be entered. With the arrival of a French fleet, the garrison surrendered and were made galley slaves.

Archbishop John Hamilton supported Mary Queen of Scots, but was hanged in 1571, having been accused of being involved in the murders of Darnley and the Regent Moray. Archbishop James Sharp was a Protestant bishop, but unpopular with Covenanters, and he was brutally murdered in front of his daughter at Magus Moor in 1679.

St Andrews Castle

St Andrews Castle

The castle lost importance, and by 1654 the town council had stone removed from the castle to repair the harbour.

The ghost of Archbishop John Hamilton, who was hanged at Stirling, is said to haunt the castle; some reports have Cardinal David Beaton's apparition. There are also tales of a White Lady, seen near the stronghold and on the nearby beach, possibly the same apparition seen more often at the cathedral.

St Andrews Cathedral, once the largest and most impressive church in Scotland, is now reduced to a very picturesque ruin, with many points of interest including St Rule's Tower, the precinct wall, cloister museum and many old burial markers.

52 miles north-east of Edinburgh, 13 miles south-east of Dundee, in St Andrews, to north of town on the sea, north of A91, west of the cathedral, the Scores, at St Andrews Castle (signposted).
NO 513169 OS: 59 KY16 9AR
Historic Scotland: castle and cathedral: open Apr-Sep, daily 9.30-17.30; Oct-Mar, daily 9.30-16.30; closed 25/26 Dec & check New Year as may be open.
Tel: 01334 477196 Web: www.historic-scotland.gov.uk
Features: Parking nearby. Shop. WC. Partial disabled access. Admission charged. Joint ticket with St Andrews Cathedral available.
Nearest:
Hill of Tarvit (10 miles)
Kellie Castle (11 miles)
Falkland Palace (21 miles)
Glamis Castle (25 miles)
Lochleven Castle (31 miles)

STIRLING CASTLE

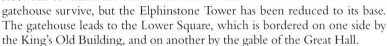

Colour photos page C60

One of the most important and powerful castles in Scotland, Stirling Castle stands on a high rock, and consists of a courtyard castle, which dates in part from the 12th century.

The castle is entered through the 18th-century outer defences and 16th-century forework of which the Prince's Tower and the gatehouse survive, but the Elphinstone Tower has been reduced to its base. The gatehouse leads to the Lower Square, which is bordered on one side by the King's Old Building, and on another by the gable of the Great Hall.

The King's Old Building contained royal chambers over a vaulted basement, reached by a turnpike stair.

A road leads between the King's Old Buildings and the hall to the Upper Square. The Chapel Royal is built on one side of the square, as is the Great Hall, which was completed during the reign of James IV. The Hall has five fireplaces, and had a magnificent hammer-beam ceiling – which had not survived, but has been replaced.

Other features of interest are the kitchens, the wall walk and the nearby King's Knot, an ornamental garden, which once had a pleasure canal.

The earliest recorded castle at Stirling was used by Malcolm Canmore in the 11th century. Alexander I died here in 1124, as did William the Lyon in

Stirling Castle

Stirling Castle, Great Hall

1214. Edward I of England captured the castle in 1304 when he used – after the garrison had surrendered – a siege engine called the War Wolf: he wanted to see if it would have worked. William Wallace took the castle for the Scots, but it was retaken by the English until the Battle of Bannockburn in 1314.

Robert the Bruce had the castle slighted, but it was rebuilt by Edward III of England, after his victory of Halidon Hill in 1333, in support of Edward Balliol. The English garrison was besieged in 1337 by Andrew Moray, but it was not until 1342 that the Scots recovered the castle.

James I had Murdoch Duke of Albany and his sons executed at the castle in 1425, James II was born here in 1430, as was James III in 1451. James II lured William, 8th Earl of Douglas, to the castle in 1452, murdered him, and had his body tossed out of one of the windows, despite promising him safe conduct. Mary, Queen of Scots, was crowned in the old chapel in 1543, and James VI was baptised here in 1566. He also stayed here in 1617, as did Charles I in 1633, and Charles II in 1650. In 1651 the castle was besieged by Monck for Cromwell, but it surrendered after a few days because of a mutiny in the garrison.

The castle was in a poor state of repair in the 18th century, but the garrison harried the Jacobites during both the 1715 and 1745 Risings, and the Jacobites besieged the castle after the Battle of Falkirk in 1746, although not very successfully.

The interior of the Royal Palace has been refurbished to return it to how it

Stirling Castle

would have looked in the medieval period. Features of the castle include the Chapel Royal, exhibition of life in the royal palace, introductory display, and the medieval kitchen display. The Museum of Argyll and Sutherland Highlanders tells the story of the regiment from 1794 to the present day.

The Pink Lady, the apparition of a beautiful woman, has reputedly been seen at the castle, and may be the ghost of Mary, Queen of Scots. Another story is that she is the ghost of a woman searching for her husband, who was killed when the castle was captured by Edward I of England in 1303. The Green Lady's appearance is a harbinger of ill news, often associated with fire. She may have been one of the ladies of Mary, Queen of Scots, and has reportedly been seen in recent times. There are also many reports of ghostly footsteps in more than one area of the castle.

Other historic places in Stirling to visit include Argyll's Lodging, at the top of Castle Wynd, an excellent example of a 17th-century town house and held by the Campbells of Argyll; Mar's Wark, the ruinous but fabulously ornate house of the Earls of Mar; the Church of the Holy Rude, dating from the 16th century and used for the coronation of James VI; and Cowane's Hospital, a memorable edifice built to house merchants who had fallen on hard times.

29 miles north-east of Glasgow, 40 miles west and north of Edinburgh, in Stirling, at Stirling Castle (signposted).
NS 790940 OS: 57 FK8 1EJ
Historic Scotland: open all year: Apr-Sep daily 9.30-18.00; Oct-Mar daily 9.30-17.00; closed 25/26 Dec; open 1/2 Jan: tel for opening times.
Tel: 01786 450000 Web: www.stirlingcastle.gov.uk
Features: Parking. Shops. Cafe. WC. Disabled access. Admission charged. Park and ride service from Broad Street.
Nearest:
Doune Castle (8 miles)
Castle Campbell (14 miles)
Callendar House (14 miles)
Drummond Castle Gardens (20 miles)
The Binns (26 miles)

TANTALLON CASTLE

Colour photos page C61

A once mighty but now shattered yet impressive ruin, Tantallon Castle is a massive 14th-century courtyard castle. It has a hugely thick 50-foot-high curtain wall, blocking off a steep coastal promontory, the sea and the height of the cliffs defending the three other sides. In front of the wall is a deep ditch, and at each end are ruined towers: one round, one D-shaped. The shell of a massive tower-gatehouse stands at the middle of the wall, and rises to six storeys. Within the castle walls are the remains of a range of buildings, which contained a hall and private chambers. There is also a deep well, and the foundations of a sea gate.

Further earthworks form the outer bailey, which has a small stone gatehouse and a 17th-century doocot. A ravelin, a triangular artillery earthwork, was constructed beyond the outer bailey, and there was a large castleton.

The castle was built by William Douglas, 1st Earl of Douglas, in about 1350. William waylaid and slew his godfather, another William Douglas, the infamous Knight of Liddesdale, and secured his position as the most powerful lord in the Borders.

George Douglas, his son, became Earl of Angus, the first of the Red Douglases, and married Mary, second daughter of Robert II. He was captured at the Battle of Homildon Hill in 1402, and died the next year. James, 3rd Earl,

Tantallon Castle

182

Tantallon Castle

used Tantallon to pursue a vendetta against the rival branch of the family, the Black Douglases. His brother, George, later 4th Earl, and James II's army routed Black Douglas forces at Arkinholm in 1455, and he was rewarded with the lordship of Douglas. He died in 1463.

Archibald, 5th Earl, better known as Bell-the-Cat, hanged James III's favourites, including Robert Cochrane, from the bridge at Lauder. He entered into a treasonable pact with Henry VII of England, which led to James IV besieging Tantallon in 1491. In 1513 Archibald died, and his two sons were killed at the Battle of Flodden.

His grandson, another Archibald, succeeded as 6th Earl of Angus. In 1514 he married Margaret Tudor, widow of James IV and sister of Henry VIII. In 1528, after many dubious ventures, Archibald had to flee to Tantallon, and James V besieged the castle with artillery. After 20 days, the king was forced to abandon the attack. Douglas retired to England, and the castle passed into the hands of the King. When James V died in 1542, Angus returned, and again took possession of Tantallon. By 1543 England and Scotland were at war, and Archibald offered to surrender the castle to the English. However, during the invasion, the English desecrated the Douglas tombs at Melrose Abbey, and Archibald changed sides and led the Scots to victory at the Battle of Ancrum Moor in 1545. He also led the Scots, along with the Earl of Hamilton, to defeat at the much more decisive Battle of Pinkie in 1547. Cannons at Tantallon took part in a naval battle between English and French fleets. Archibald died at the castle in 1556 .

Mary, Queen of Scots, visited in 1566. Archibald, 8th Earl, entered into more treasonable negotiations with the English, and had to go into exile in 1581. He died in England in 1588, as a result – it was said – of a spell cast by

Tantallon Castle

Agnes Sampson, who was later condemned as a witch by James VI and burnt. William, 9th Earl, died in 1591, and the 10th Earl, another William, was a staunch Catholic, who was also forced into exile to die in France in 1611. His son, again William, 11th Earl, also became Marquis of Douglas. Tantallon was seized by Covenanters in 1639.

In 1650 moss troopers, based at the castle, did so much damage to Cromwell's lines of communication that in 1651 he sent an army to attack Tantallon. The bombardment lasted 12 days and destroyed so much of the old stronghold that the garrison surrendered.

The castle was then abandoned as a fortress and residence, and in 1699 the property was sold, along with the Barony of North Berwick, to the Dalrymples.

31 miles east of Edinburgh, 3.5 miles east of North Berwick, off A198, on southern shore of Firth of Forth, at Tantallon Castle (signposted). NT 596851   OS: 67   EH39 5PN
Historic Scotland: open Apr-Sep, daily 9.30-17.30; Oct-Mar, daily 9.30-16.30; closed 25/26 Dec and 1/2 Jan; last ticket sold 30 mins before closing. Tel: 01620 892727   Web: www.historic-scotland.gov.uk
Features: Parking (walk to castle). Shop. Refreshments. WC. Limited disabled access. Admission charged.
Nearest:
Dirleton Castle (5 miles)
Crichton Castle (27 miles)
Newhailes (27 miles)
Craigmillar Castle (29 miles)
Palace of Holyroodhouse (30 miles)

THE BINNS

Colour photo page C59

THE BINNS
Linlithgow ● ● Edinburgh

Standing on the site of an old castle, The Binns, a castellated mansion of three storeys washed in a delicate pink, was built between 1612 and 1630, with additions later in the 17th century, in the 1740s, and in the 1820s. The house has fine plaster ceilings from the 17th century, and stands in 260 acres of landscaped parkland with peacocks overlooking the Forth.

This was a property of the Livingstones of Kilsyth, but was sold to the Dalziels in 1612. General Tom Dalyell of The Binns was taken prisoner in 1651 at the Battle of Worcester – when an army under Charles II was defeated by Cromwell – but escaped from the Tower of London, and joined the Royalist rising of 1654. He went into exile when the rising collapsed, and served in the Russian army with the Tsar's cossacks, when he is reputed to have roasted prisoners over open fires, and then to have introduced thumbscrews to Scotland. Returning after the Restoration, Dalziel was made commander of forces in Scotland from 1666 to 1685. He led the force that defeated the Covenanters at the Battle of Rullion Green in 1666, and raised the Royal Scots Greys here in 1681.

The Dalziels are buried in a vault at Abercorn Church, including Tam.

The Binns

The Binns

The present attractive church, which is dedicated to St Serf, dates from the Reformation to the present day, and is open to the public.

The house and grounds are reputedly haunted by the ghost of Tam Dalyell, which is said to sometimes be seen on a white horse riding up to the castle. His boots, which are on display, are said to vanish when his spirit is abroad. Another ghost, said to haunt the grounds, is that of an old man gathering firewood.

There is also a story of a tunnel leading down from The Binns to Blackness Castle.

38 miles east of Glasgow, 15 miles west of Edinburgh, 4 miles east and north of Linlithgow, off A904, at The Binns (signposted).
NT 051785 OS: 65 EH49 7NA
NTS: House open for guided tours Jun-Sep, Sat-Wed 14.00-17.00 (last at 16.15), closed Thu & Fri; parkland open all year, gates close at 19.30.
Tel: 0844 493 2127 Web: www.nts.org.uk
Features: Parking. WC. Parkland. Picnic area. Disabled access to ground floor. Admission charged.
Nearest:
Blackness Castle (2 miles)
Linlithgow Palace (4 miles)
Hopetoun House (8 miles (by road))
Lauriston Castle (12 miles)
Callendar House (13 miles)

THIRLESTANE CASTLE

Colour photo page C62

A magnificent building in a fine setting, Thirlestane Castle is a 16th-century castle, the oldest part of which is a rectangular tower house or block of three storeys, which had large round towers at each corner. The castle was considerably enlarged in the 1670s by Sir William Bruce and Robert Mylne, with the rebuilding of the main block, heightening it to six storeys, and the addition of round turrets. Three semi-circular towers along each side contain stairs, as do many of the turrets. Parapets are supported on arches running along each side. A symmetrical forecourt was also added, with three-storey wings, which were extended in the 19th century. The 19th-century extensions were designed by the architect William Burn, and possibly David Bryce.

A fine 17th-century plaster ceiling survives on the second floor, as do Baroque plaster ceilings elsewhere, and the castle has a sumptuous interior.

The original stronghold of the Maitlands stood two miles away at Old Thirlestane. The present castle was built by Sir John Maitland, James VI's chancellor, but it was John Maitland, Duke of Lauderdale, a very powerful man in Scotland in the 17th century, who had the present house remodelled

Thirlestane Castle

Thirlestane Castle

by Sir William Bruce. Lauderdale was Secretary of State for Scotland from 1661–80, but he was eventually replaced after the Covenanter uprising which ended with their defeat at the Battle of Bothwell Brig. His ghost is said to haunt Thirlestane, as well as St Mary's Parish Church in Haddington where he is interred.

Bonnie Prince Charlie stayed here in 1745 on his way south during the Jacobite Rising.

Dry rot was recently found in the castle, and the building is in the process of being renovated in 2013, and into 2014.

28 miles south-east of Edinburgh, 70 miles east of Glasgow, just north-east of Lauder, off A68, at Thirlestane Castle (signposted).
NT 540473   OS: 73   TD2 6RU
Check with castle as closed in 2013 and not clear when will reopen in 2014; grounds open all year.
Tel: 01578 722430   Web: www.thirlestanecastle.co.uk
Features: Parking. Garden and grounds. Adventure playground. Admission charged.
Nearest:
Mellerstain (12 mile)
Abbotsford (14 miles)
Crichton Castle (16 miles)
Floors Castle (17 miles)
Bowhill House (21 miles)

THREAVE CASTLE

Colour photo page C62

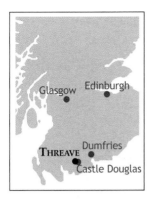

Lurking on an island in the River Dee, Threave Castle consists of a massive, strong and very impressive 14th-century tower, rectangular in plan, of five storeys and formerly a garret. This stood within a courtyard, which was enclosed by a wall and ditch, with drum towers designed for artillery at each corner, only one of which survives. An impressive gateway remains in the curtain-wall.

Threave Castle

Threave Castle

The entrance to the main tower, at entresol level, was by a bridge from the gatehouse in the curtain wall. A kitchen, with a fireplace, occupied the upper part of the vaulted basement. The chamber beneath contains a well and a deep pit-prison entered by a trapdoor.

An earlier stronghold here was burnt by Edward Bruce in 1308. The present castle was started by Archibald the Grim – so named because his face was terrible to look upon in battle – 3rd Earl of Douglas, and Lord of Galloway from 1369 until 1390. He died at Threave in 1400. His son, Archibald, married James I's sister and was created Duke of Tourraine in France after winning the Battle of Baugé against the English in 1421. He did not have very long to enjoy his title as he was killed by the English at the Battle of Verneuil in 1424.

It was from Threave that William, the young 6th Earl, and David his brother rode to Edinburgh Castle in 1440 for the Black Dinner, where they were taken out and summarily executed. The 8th Earl, another William, was murdered in 1452 by James II at Stirling, after being invited there as an act of reconciliation. James, 9th Earl, was rather hostile to the king after the brutal murder and plotted with the English.

In 1455, following the defeat of Douglas and his family the Black Douglases, James II besieged Threave with artillery. The king was helped by the MacLellans: Sir Patrick MacLellan of Bombie, was murdered by beheading at Threave in

1452 by the Earl of Douglas. The garrison surrendered, but this seems to have been achieved as much by bribery as by ordinance.

Threave then became a Royal fortress. In 1513 the Maxwells were made keepers, and in 1525 the post was made hereditary. After being captured at the Battle of Solway Moss in 1542, the Maxwell keeper was obliged to turn the castle over to the English, but it was retrieved by the Earl of Arran in 1545.

In 1640 the castle was besieged by an army of Covenanters for 13 weeks until it was forced to surrender. The castle was slighted and partly dismantled. Threave was reputedly used as a prison for French troops during the Napoleonic wars.

86 miles south of Glasgow, 97 miles south and west of Edinburgh, 22 miles south-west of Dumfries, 2 miles west of Castle Douglas, off A75, then foot and short boat trip to Threave Island in the River Dee. NX 739623 OS: 84 DG7 1TJ
Historic Scotland: open Apr-Sep, daily 9.30-16.30 (last outward sailing), Oct, daily 9.30-15.30 (last outward sailing). Owned by NTS; administered by Historic Scotland. 0.5 miles walk to ferry.
Tel: 07711 223101 (mobile) Web: www.historic-scotland.gov.uk
Features: Parking. Sales Area. WC (car park). Picnic area. Limited disabled access to island. Admission charged.
Nearest:
Cardoness Castle (13 miles)
Caerlaverock Castle (28 miles)
Drumlanrig Castle (34 miles)
Dumfries House (51 miles)
Culzean Castle (54 miles)

TOLQUHON CASTLE

Colour photos page C63

Once a strong but comfortable fortress, Tolquhon Castle is a fine building, and consists of a strong ruined 15th-century tower in one corner of a courtyard enclosed by ranges of buildings, including a drum-towered gatehouse. A large round tower stands at one corner, with a square tower at the opposite side. The walls are pierced by gunloops.

The main three-storey block, opposite the old tower, has a projecting semi-circular stair-tower crowned by a square caphouse. The entrance leads into a long vaulted passage, which opens into three vaulted cellars: a wine-cellar, the kitchen with a wide-arched fireplace, and a bakehouse. Both kitchen and wine-cellar have small stairs to the hall above. There is also a pit-prison.

The first floor was reached by a wide curved stair. The hall has a large moulded fireplace and is paved by hexagonal flagstones. An adjoining secret chamber was reached by a trapdoor from above.

The gatehouse range has two round towers and an arched pend, which was defended by shot-holes. The original iron yetts survive.

The first tower was built by the Prestons of Craigmillar, but the property passed by marriage to the Forbes family in 1420, who built the rest of the castle. Sir Alexander Forbes, 6th Laird, died at the Battle of Pinkie in 1547, while William, 7th Laird, built the castle as it now is and died in 1596 – his carved tomb, along with his wife Elizabeth Gordon, survives in Tarves kirkyard. James VI visited in 1589, during his campaign against the Gordon Earl of Huntly. The 10th laird, another Sir Alexander, saved Charles II's life at the Battle of Worcester in 1651.

Tolquhon Castle

Tolquhon Castle

The Forbeses sold the property to the Farquhars in 1716 because of debts
from involvement in the Darien Scheme, although William Forbes, 11th Laird,
had to be forcibly removed from the castle in 1718 by a detachment of soldiers.
Later part of the castle was used as a farmhouse, but this was abandoned around
the end of the 19th century.

There are reports of sightings of a White Lady, reputedly seen unmoving at
the top of a staircase. Accounts have also been recorded of a Grey Lady,
apparently seen wandering in the ruins at midnight, with the sound of groaning.

143 miles north and east of Edinburgh, 17 miles north of Aberdeen,
7 miles east of Oldmeldrum, off B999 1 mile north of junction with
A920, at Tolquhon Castle (signposted).
NJ 873286 OS: 38 AB41 7LP
Historic Scotland: Open Apr-Sep, daily 9.30-17.30; last ticket sold 30
mins before closing.
Tel: 01651 851286 Web: www.historic-scotland.gov.uk
Features: Parking. Sales area. Picnic area. WC. Disabled limited access
and WC. Admission charged.
Nearest:
Haddo House (5 miles)
Fyvie Castle (13 miles)
Castle Fraser (21 miles)
Delgatie (23 miles)
Huntly (30 miles)

TRAQUAIR HOUSE

Colour photos page C64

T he oldest continuously inhabited house in Scotland, Traquair House is an impressive altered and extended tower house, which had its origins as early as the 12th century. The oldest identifiable part can still be seen to the left of the main block, which was then extended between 1500 and 1600. The two wings were added by the architect James Smith in 1694, and he also designed the courtyard and wrought-iron railings. There are no additions or alterations after this date. The walls are whitewashed, and there are turrets and dormer windows, as well as a priest's cell, on the top floor, complete with secret stair.

Traquair originated as a royal hunting lodge and was reputedly visited by 27 Scottish monarchs, and some of England, including Edward I and Edward II in the 14th century. The lands had passed to the Douglases by the 13th century, then went through several families, until sold to the Stewart Earls of Buchan in 1478. James, the then laird of Traquair, was killed at the Battle of Flodden in 1513.

Mary, Queen of Scots, visited with Lord Darnley in 1566. She left behind a quilt, possibly embroidered by herself and her Four Marys, and reputedly the cradle where the infant James VI slept during the visit. John Stewart, 4th Laird, who had been the captain of the Queen's bodyguard, helped her escape from Lochleven Castle after her 'abdication' in 1568. The bed where she slept some

Traquair House

194

Traquair House, King's Room

of her last nights on Scottish soil was rescued from Terregles and is at Traquair. The family were made Earls of Traquair in 1633.

Bonnie Prince Charlie visited the house on his way south in 1745 to invade England. He entered Traquair through the famous Bear Gates. One story is that Charles, the 5th Earl, closed and locked them after Charlie's departure, swearing they would not be unlocked until a Stewart once more sat on the throne of the country. They are still locked, and Charles was imprisoned.

The house is now home to Catherine, 21st Lady of Traquair, and lies in 100 acres of woodland and lawns with a maze and a walk to the River Tweed.

29 miles south of Edinburgh, 59 miles east and south of Glasgow, 1 mile south of Innerleithen, off B709, at Traquair House (signposted). NT 330354   OS: 73   EH44 6PW
Open early Apr-late Oct, daily: Apr-Sep, 11.00-17.00; Oct, 11.00-16.00; Nov, open Sat & Sun only, 11.00-15.00; luxurious b&b accommodation available; weddings and events venue.
Tel: 01896 830323   Web: www.traquair.co.uk
Features: Parking. Shop. Restaurant. WC. Partial disabled access. Extensive grounds. Maze. Craft workshops. Brewery. Traquair Fair Admission charged.
Nearest:
Abbotsford (16 miles)
Bowhill House (17 miles)
Thirlestane Castle (21 miles)
Mellerstain (27 miles)
Floors Castle (28 miles)

GLOSSARY

Arcade A series of arches supported by piers or columns. A blind arcade is built against a wall

Ashlar Masonry of worked stone blocks with even faces and squared edges

Attic The top storey entirely within a gabled roof

Aumbry Originally almry, 'a place for alms'. A cupboard, usually in a stone wall

Balustrade Ornamental parapet of posts and railings

Barmkin A walled courtyard, often of modest size and defensive strength

Baroque Architectural and artistic style from Italy in the early 17th century: grand, flamboyant and extravagant

Bartizan A turret, corbelled out from a wall, usually crowning corners of a building

Basement The lowest storey of a building, sometimes below ground

Batter A slight inward inclination or tilt of a wall from its base upwards, either to add strength or to make tunnelling by attacking forces more difficult

Battlement A crenellated parapet to shoot from between the solid sections, or merlons – the crenel being the space

Bay A section or compartment of a building

Bay window A window projecting from a building at ground level, either rectangular or polygonal, of one or more storeys. If it is corbelled out above ground level, it is an oriel window

Bow window As bay window; but curved in plan

Caphouse A small watch-chamber at the top of a turnpike stair, often opening into the parapet walk and sometimes rising from within the parapet

Caponier A covered passage across a ditch of a castle from which to defend the bottom of the ditch from attack

Castle A fortified house or stronghold; the residence of a nobleman or landowner

Castellated Designed or remodelled in such a way as to look like a castle, such as with battlements, turrets and arrowslits or gunloops, but the 'defensive' features are purely decorative

Castellations Battlements and turrets

Classical Revival of classical architectural styles used by the Greeks and Romans, characterized by columns, pediments and symmetrical designs

Colonnade A series of evenly spaced columns

Corbiestepped (Scots) Squared stones forming steps upon a gable

Corbel A projecting bracket supporting other stonework or timbers

Courtyard castle Usually a castle of some size and importance built around a central courtyard, normally with a tower or keep, gatehouse, and ranges of buildings such as a kitchen, bakehouse, stable and chapel

Crenellations Battlements made up of crenels and merlons

Crowstepped Squared stones forming steps upon a gable (corbiestepped)

Curtain wall A high enclosing stone wall around a bailey

Donjon The keep or central fortress in a castle

Doocot (Scots) A dovecot

Dormer window A window standing up vertically from a slope of a roof

E-plan tower house Tower house with a main block and at least three wings at right angles, dating from the 16th and 17th centuries

Eave An overhanging edge of a roof

Entresol A low storey within two high ones (mezzanine)

Finial A projection or pinnacle crowning a window or other structure, usually decorative

Fortalice (Scots) A medium-sized fortified building

Fresco A painting done on wet plaster

Frieze A horizontal band of ornament

Gable A vertical wall or other vertical surface, frequently triangular, at the end of a pitched roof, often with a chimney. In Scotland often corbiestepped (crowstepped)

Garderobe A medieval privy, usually built into the wall of a castle

Garret The top storey of a building within the roof; attic

Gothic Non-classical medieval architecture, distinguished by high-pitched roofs, sharp-pointed arches, and narrow windows, which progressively became less severe. Revived in its various forms by the Victorians, and seen in many 19th-century mansions

Gunloop An opening for shooting firearms through with an external splay. See also shot-hole

Hall house Defensible, usually two-storey building containing a hall, usually above a basement

Hammer-beam An elaborate type of roof used in Gothic and Tudor buildings. To avoid tie-beams across an imposing hall, short timber cantilevers (or hammer-beams) were used

Harling (Scots) Wet dash, or roughcasting, hurled or dashed onto a rubble wall of a castle or house to give additional protection against the weather

Heraldic panel A stone panel with the arms and initials of a noble and his wife (using her maiden name). Often records the date, referring usually to the construction or modification of a building

House A castle, tower or fortalice, especially where these have been extended or modified; also mansion, home or dwelling etc.

Laird's lug (Scots) 'Lord's ear'. A hidden chamber from where the laird could overhear those in the hall while not being seen himself

L-plan tower house Distinctive Scottish form of the tower house in which a wing was added at right angles to the main tower block, thereby affording greater protection by covering fire and providing more accommodation. Dates from 1540 to 1680

Lancet window A slender pointed arch window

Lintel A horizontal beam of stone, bridging an opening

Loggia A covered, open arcade

Loop A small opening to admit light or for the firing of weapons

Machicolation A slot out of which stones or missiles could be shot

Main block Principal part of a castle, usually containing the hall and lord's chamber

Mezzanine A low storey between two higher ones (entresol)

Moat A ditch, water filled or dry, around an enclosure

Motte A steep-sided flat-topped mound

Motte and bailey A defence system, Roman in origin, consisting of an earth motte (mound) carrying a wooden tower with a bailey (open court) with an enclosing ditch and palisade

Moulding An ornament of continuous section

Mullion A vertical dividing beam in a window, sometimes made of stone

Murder-hole Opening in the roof of a passage, especially an entrance, through which attackers could be ambushed

Newel The centre post in a turnpike or winding stair

Niche A vertical recess in a wall, often to take a statue

Ogee A double curve, bending one way then the other

Oratory A small private domestic chapel

Oriel A bay window projecting out from a wall above ground level

Palace An old Scots term for a two-storey hall or residential block

Parapet A wall for protection at any sudden drop but defensive in a castle

Pediment A small gable over a doorway or window, especially a dormer

Pepperpot turret A bartizan with conical or pyramidal roof

Piscina A basin with a drain for washing the Communion or Mass vessels, usually set in, or against, a wall

Pit prison A dark prison only reached by a hatch in a vault

Pleasaunce, Pleasance A walled garden

Portcullis A wooden and/or iron gate designed to rise and fall in vertical grooves

Portico A porch suspended on columns over the entrance to a building

Postern A secondary gateway or doorway; a back or side entrance

Rampart A stone or earth wall surrounding a castle

Re-entrant angle Inside corner where two wings of a building meet when at right angles

Renaissance 'Rebirth'; the rediscovery of classical architecture in Italy about 1420, which then spread throughout Europe, coming to Scotland somewhat later

Rib-vault A vault supported by ribs or decorated with them

Rococo 18th-century architectural style, less flamboyant and more elegant than Baroque

Round (Scots) A roofless bartizan

Royal castle A castle held by a keeper or constable for the monarch

Scale-and-platt Stair with short straight flights and turnings at landings

Screen A wall, wooden or stone, one use of which was to divide an adjoining kitchen from the hall

Skew (Scots) Sloping or sloped stones finishing a gable higher than the roof

Shot-hole A small round hole in a wall through which weapons were fired

Slight To destroy a castle's defences to a greater or lesser extent

Spring Level at which a vault or an arch rises

Squinch A small arch built obliquely across each internal angle of a square tower or other structure to carry a turret or tower

Stoup A vessel for holy water

String-course Intermediate course, or moulding, projecting from the surface of a wall

Tempera Form of wall-painting directly on plaster or wood

Tower house Self-contained house with the main rooms stacked vertically usually with a hall over a vaulted basement with further storeys above. Normally in a small courtyard, or barmkin. Dating mainly from 1540 to about 1680

T-plan House or tower where the main (long) block has a wing or tower (usually for the stair) in the centre of one front

Turnpike stair (Scots) Spiral stair around a newel or central post

Turret A small tower usually attached to a building

Vault An arched ceiling, most usually of stone. Tunnel- or barrel-vaulting, (the simplest kind) is, in effect, a continuous arch. Pointed tunnel-vaults are found occasionally in Scottish buildings. Groin-vaults have four curving triangular surfaces created by the intersection of two tunnel-vaults at right-angles. Also see Rib-vault

Yett A strong hinged gate made of interwoven iron bars

Wall-walk A walkway on top of a wall, protected by a parapet

Z-plan Distinctive Scottish form of the tower house whereby two corner towers were added to the main tower block at diagonally opposite corners, thereby affording greater protection by covering fire and providing more accommodation. Dates from the 16th and 17th centuries

TITLES AND OFFICES

Abbot The head of an abbey, a religious house of higher standing than a priory.

Archbishop A bishop of the highest rank; created in Scotland in 1472 (St Andrews), and then in 1492 (Glasgow).

Baron Originally a land-holding noble; now the second lowest rank of title in Great Britain.

Baronet The lowest rank of title in Great Britain; in Scotland many families were made Baronets of Nova Scotia (a colony in Canada) from 1625 until about 1714.

Bishop A clergyman having spiritual and administrative control over a diocese or area; in Scotland in medieval times there were bishops of St Andrews, Glasgow, Galloway, Dunblane, Dunkeld, Brechin, Aberdeen, Moray, the Isles, Caithness, and Orkney (also see **Archbishop** and **Cardinal**).

Cardinal A member of the Sacred College of the Catholic Church, ranking next to the Pope; the most famous person holding the office in earlier times was Cardinal David Beaton, Archbishop of St Andrews, who was murdered in 1546.

Chamberlain The chief financial officer or administrative officer, and on record from the 12th century; the office holder was a layman and duties included supervising royal burghs, but the financial duties were later divided between the **Treasurer** and the **Comptroller**; the importance of the

office diminished from the 15th century although it continued until 1705.

Chancellor An office, first on record from the 12th century, who was in charge of the Great Seal (also see **Keeper of the Great Seal**); until 1335 the Chancellor was a cleric; in the 16th and 17th centuries the head of the civil administration in Scotland under the monarch; also the head of a university.

Commendator Originally a churchman appointed to administer (and use the revenues from) an abbey, priory, bishopric or other benefice that the holder was not qualified to hold; in the 16th century used by laymen to enjoy the revenues of Church property without performing any religious duties.

Comptroller 'Roller of Accounts' (or controller of royal finances), and on record from the 13th century; the office was responsible for financial control of the royal household and gathered rents from crown lands and shared responsibilities with those of the **Treasurer**.

Constable of Scotland The office is on record from the 12th century; duties included organising the monarch's forces during times of war and keeping peace at court; long held by the Hay, Earls of Errol.

Countess The female equivalent or wife of an **Earl**.

Duke A noble of the highest rank, beneath the monarch; the first Dukedom in Scotland was created in

1398 for David, son of Robert III; the title is currently held by Prince Charles; **Marquis/Marquess** is the next title in descending order.

Earl A title equivalent to a count or mormaer (rulers or lesser kings of an area beneath the monarch or high king) or Norse Jarl; this became translated to the English Earl; reputedly there were originally seven earldoms or provinces in the early kingdom of Scots: Angus, Atholl, Strathearn, Fife, Mar, Moray and Caithness; others were created from the 12th century onwards; in the British peerage the title is higher in rank than **Viscount** and lower than **Marquis/Marquess;** there is no female equivalent of Earl so the term **Countess** is used.

Great Steward of Scotland *see* **Steward**

High Steward *see* **Steward**

Justiciar The office is on record from the 12th century, and the holder was the chief legal and political officer and supervised the work of the **Sheriffs** and heard any appeals; the office was eventually subsumed into that of the **Justice General.** There were two nobles holding the office, one for north of the Forth and one for the south of the Forth.

Justice General The chief judge in criminal cases, and the office was held by several families until being held by the Campbells of Argyll from 1514 until 1628. After 1672 the office was held by a professional lawyer, and it was joined with **Lord President** in 1837.

Keeper of the Great Seal The Great Seal (a metal mould for producing wax seals) allowed charters to be ratified by the monarch without having to individually sign each document; the office of keeper was held by many different individuals down the centuries, but it is now held by the First Minister of the Scottish Parliament.

Keeper of the Privy Seal of Scotland The office is first on record from the 14th century. The office was held by many different individuals down the centuries but there has been no appointment since 1922.

King The ruler or head of an independent state; in Scotland the first recognised King of Scots was Kenneth MacAlpin, who came to power around 843, although the kingdoms of Scots and of Picts which he united had had one king on more than one occasion before then. Scotland remained an independent kingdom with its own monarchs for much of the following time (a notable exception being the run up to the Wars of Independence after the death of Alexander III in 1290) until the crowns of Scotland and England were united by James VI, King of Scots, in 1603.

Knight A gentleman invested by a king or high lord with the military and social standing of this rank; the person knighted used the title 'Sir'.

Lady-in-waiting A lady of the royal household who attends a queen or princess.

Laird Scot's word for lord, often used to denote a smaller landowner.

Lord A male member of the nobility or one who has power or ownership of land or some other office.

Lord Advocate The chief law office of the monarch who has discretion over prosecution and could give advice on legal matters; the office was established in 1478 and survives until this day, the holder now being the chief law officer to the Scottish Parliament.

Lord High Commissioner On record from the 12th century and the representative of the monarch, who attended both the Scottish Parliament and the General Assembly of the Church of Scotland, although only this latter duty now applies. Some of the duties of the office were similar and at times taken over by the **Keeper of the Great Seal**. The office has not been filled since the 18th century, the last holder being James Ogilvie, Earl of Seafield, who died in 1730.

Lord Lyon King of Arms *see* **Lyon King of Arms**

Lord of the Isles A title taken by the MacDonalds in the 13th century as they controlled much of the western seaboard of Scotland. It was not officially recognised by the kings of Scots until the 15th century, but James IV imprisoned the last Lord in 1493 and the title is now one of those held by the heir to the British throne, Prince Charles.

Lord President (of the Court of Session) The presiding judge of the Court of Session (the highest court in Scotland) since 1532 and still in existence. The office was originally only held by a cleric but this was abolished in 1579; the office was combined with that of the **Justice General** in 1837.

Lord of Session Originally one of the fifteen judges of the Court of Session (see **Lord President** above). Numbers were increased in recent times; the Lords of Session can also preside in the High Court.

Lyon King of Arms Office, first on record from the 14th century, which has ultimate jurisdiction for matters armorial and heraldic. There is a Public Register of all arms and bearings from 1672, and there are several Heralds and Pursuivants associated with the office.

Marischal Office, on record from the 12th century, which was long held by the Keith family, Earls Marischal from 1458, although the Keiths were forfeited following the 1715 Jacobite Rising.

Marchioness The female equivalent or wife of a **Marquis/Marquess**.

Marquess The second highest rank of nobility in the British peerage, between a **Duke** and an **Earl**. **Equivalent** to the **Marquis** in the Scottish peerage.

Marquis The second highest rank of nobility in the Scottish peerage, between a **Duke** and an **Earl**. **Marquess** is equivalent in the British peerage; Marquis was used in Scotland, France and elsewhere.

Master of the Household An important office, essentially combining the duties of the High Steward, Comptroller and Treasurer. Long held by the Dukes of Argyll in Scotland and created by James I in the 15th century.

Mormaer *see* **Earl**

Preceptor The head of a preceptory, the religious house of an order of holy knights. The Knights Templar were established in Scotland, but when they were suppressed by the Pope in 1320 their property went to the Knights of St John, who were based at Torphichen in central Scotland and the last of whom, before the Reformation, was Sir James Sandilands.

Prior The head of a priory, a religious house of less standing than (and dependant upon) an abbey or cathedral.

Queen The female equivalent of or wife of a King, The only woman to rule Scotland as an independent kingdom in her own right was Mary, Queen of Scots.

Sheriff Originally (from the 12th century) the office was concerned with financial and civil administration of an area as well as the hearing of appeals from barony courts. From the later medieval period the office became hereditary but this was abolished in 1747. In Scotland Sheriff Courts have jurisdiction in most areas except for the most serious of crimes such as rape, murder and treason, which are tried at the High Court (of Justiciary), while appeals are held at the Court of Session.

Standard Bearer The holder had the privilege of bearing the Scottish standard into battle; hereditary office, held by the Scrymgeour family, later Earls of Dundee, from the time of

William Wallace. This was disputed by the Earls of Lauderdale and a separate office was established for them in the 19th century called Bearer of the National Flag of Scotland.

Steward (of Scotland) Office held by Walter Fitzalan from the middle of the 12th century and then by his descendants. Responsibilities included being the chief of the royal household, collecting taxes, administering justice and the High Steward was also next in power to the king during time of war. Robert, son of Walter the High Steward and Marjorie, daughter of Robert the Bruce, became Robert II, King of Scots, in 1371. The title of High Steward was given to the heir to the monarch and is currently one of the titles held by Prince Charles.

Thane The term was used in Scotland from the 12th century, and was a landowner or head of a family, although of lesser rank than an **Earl** (or Mormaer)**.**

Treasurer An office sharing financial administration of Scotland along with the **Comptroller**; responsibilities included managing crown expenses not involved with the royal household.

Viscount Rank of nobility between a **Baron** and an **Earl**.

Index of Castles and Stately Homes

The number following the castle or house is the first page of the entry in the main text followed by the page number of the photo or photos in the colour section. HS are properties managed by Historic Scotland, while NTS are properties managed by The National Trust for Scotland.